ESCAPE
&
THE MAN WHO QUESTIONS DEATH

ESCAPE

&

THE MAN WHO QUESTIONS DEATH

Gao Xingjian

Translated by Gilbert C. F. Fong

The Chinese University Press

Escape *and* The Man Who Questions Death
  By Gao Xingjian
  Translated by Gilbert C. F. Fong

ISBN-10: 962–996–308–6
ISBN-13: 978–962–996–308–8

THE CHINESE UNIVERSITY PRESS
The Chinese University of Hong Kong
Sha Tin, N. T., Hong Kong
Fax: +852 2603 6692
    +852 2603 7355
E-mail: cup@cuhk.edu.hk
Web-site: www.chineseupress.com

Printed in Hong Kong

The work described in this book is part of the result of "The Gao Xingjian
Project" which was fully supported by the Earmarked Research Grant dispensed
by the Research Grants Council of the Hong Kong Special Administrative Region
(Project no.: CUHK 4119/03H)

Contents

Introduction

Two Autobiographical Plays by Gao Xingjian

Mabel Lee
University of Sydney

Gao Xingjian (b. 1940 in Ganzhou, Jiangxi Province, China) established his credentials in Chinese literary circles with the sensational staging of three plays, namely, *Juedui xinhao* 絕對信號 (1982; tr. as *Alarm Signal*, 1996), *Chezhan* 車站 (1983; tr. as *The Bus Stop*, 1996; also tr. as *Bus Stop*, 1998), and *Yeren* 野人 (1985; tr. as *Wild Man*, 1990), at the People's Art Theater in Beijing. The Cultural Revolution (1966–1976) and the persecution of writers had ended, yet politics continued to intrude upon literature. Gao's plays and his other writings, particularly his book *Xiandai xiaoshuo jiqiao chutan* 現代小説技巧 初探 [Preliminary exploration into the art of modern fiction] (1981, repr. 1982), audaciously challenged the socialist–realist literary guidelines established in Yan'an by Mao Zedong in 1942, and he became one of the first victims in the Oppose Spiritual Pollution campaign that lasted for several months in 1983. *Bus Stop* and *Preliminary Exploration Into the Art of Modern Fiction* were banned, his name was circulated on a blacklist to publishers, and he was denounced for promoting the modernist literature of the "decadent capitalist West."

The campaign petered out toward the end of 1983, and Gao's manuscripts that had been shelved for several months by editors began to appear in literary magazines from early 1984. For two decades of his adult life he had been writing in secret because what he wrote contravened Mao Zedong's guidelines for literary production that had been institutionalized with the founding of the People's Republic of China in 1949. During the Cultural Revolution he had burned a suitcase of manuscripts, including ten plays, and a large number of short stories, poems, and essays, rather than risk having them found and used as evidence against him. When the Cultural Revolution ended and it was possible for him to publish for the first time, he was no longer able to restrain his intense craving to fulfill his creative impulses. In the space of eight years (1980–1988) he published ten plays, as well as numerous short stories, essays on drama, critiques on modern Western literature, and his translations of Jacques Prévert's *Paroles* (1984) and Eugene Ionesco's *La Cantatrice chauve* (1985). In the same period he also published four books: *Preliminary Exploration into the Art of Modern Fiction*, a novella *You zhi gezi jiao Hongchunr* 有隻鴿子叫紅唇兒 [A pigeon called Red Beak] (1984), *Gao Xingjian xiju ji* 高行健戲劇集 [Collected plays by Gao Xingjian] (1985), and *Dui yizhong xiandai xiju de zhuiqiu* 對一種現代戲劇的追求 [In search of modern theater] (1988). However, certain custodians of Mao's guidelines for literature in the Chinese Writers' Association continued a personal vendetta against him that culminated in the banning of his play *Bi'an* 彼岸 (1986; tr. as *The Other Side*, 1997; also tr. as *The Other Shore*, 1999) during rehearsals in 1986.

Gao relocated to Paris at the end of 1987 where he was able to devote himself to purely creative activities with a sense of freedom he had not experienced since childhood. A highly talented artist, he was able to sustain his literary activities by selling his Chinese ink paintings, and before long began to make his mark in the art world through exhibitions of his artworks and the publication of his writings on aesthetics. His fiction in this period include his two autobiographical novels, *Lingshan* 靈山 (1990; tr. as *Soul Mountain*, 2000) and *Yige ren de shengjing* 一個人的聖經 (1999; tr. as *One Man's Bible*, 2002), and a collection of seventeen short stories *Gei wo laoye mai yugan* 給我老爺買魚竿 (1989; tr. as *Buying a Fishing Rod for My Grandfather*, 2004). However, as he had virtually completed his manuscript of *Soul Mountain* in China, and the stories of *Buying a Fishing Rod for My Grandfather* had previously been published in various Chinese literary magazines, apart from writing *One Man's Bible* over the three years 1997–1999, painting, and writing the essays collected in *Meiyou zhuyi* 沒有主義 [Without isms] (1996), the remainder of his time was almost exclusively devoted to writing new plays, play production, and, increasingly, to directing his plays.

In Paris Gao wrote (in a couple of instances revised) the plays contained in *Gao Xingjian xiju liuzhong* 高行健戲劇六種 [Six volumes of plays by Gao Xingjian] (1995): *The Other Shore*, *Mingcheng* 冥城 [Netherworld] (1995), *Shanhai jing zhuan* 山海經傳 [Romance of the *Classic of Mountains and Seas*] (1993), *Taowang* 逃亡 (1990; tr. as *Fugitives*, 1993; also tr. as *Escape*, 2007), *Sheng-si jie* 生死界 (1991; tr. as *Between Life and Death*, 1999 and 2005), *Yeyou shen* 夜遊神 (1995; tr. as *Nocturnal Wanderer*, 1999), and *Duihua yu fanjie* 對話與反詰 (1993; tr. as *Dialogue and Rebuttal*, 1999). He also wrote the play *Zhoumo sichongzou* 週末四重奏 (1996; tr. as *Weekend Quartet*, 1999), the modern Peking Opera *Bayue xue* 八月雪 (2000; tr. as *Snow in August*, 2003), and the play *Kouwen siwang* 叩問死亡 (2004; tr. as *The Man Who Questions Death*, 2007). In the same period, he also wrote the French versions of four of those plays: *Au bord de la vie* (1993), *Le somnambule* (1995), *Quatre quatuors pour un weekend* (1998), and *Le Quêteur de la Mort* (2003).

In 2000, when Gao was awarded the Nobel Prize for Literature—the first time the Prize had been awarded for a body of works written in the Chinese language—his major works had been published in Chinese, French, Swedish, and English; and his plays had been staged in China, Yugoslavia, France, Sweden, Austria, Poland, Germany, Japan, Australia, Italy, Romania, Taiwan, Hong Kong, Ivory Coast, and the United States. Gao has a solid knowledge of Eastern and Western theater traditions and practices, and his interest extends beyond the writing of the play to all aspects of theater production, including directing, choreography, lighting, sound effects, props, and even the training of the actors. He is committed to creating a modern theater aesthetics that will return theatricality to theater, and his plays characteristically contain touches of humor and the absurd that are subtle and elegant, yet highly powerful. His strong intellect is reflected in his plays, and, importantly, his artistic genius allows him to visually conceptualize—as in cinematic film—every frame of the events to occur on stage.

While in China it was Gao's aversion to the straitjacket of socialist–realist conventions imposed on literary production that had led him onto a track of ongoing exploration into how to gratify his own highly developed intellectual and aesthetic sensibilities as a writer and artist. Having relocated to Paris he was able to write and paint without the restraints of politics, but soon found himself confronted by the insidious challenges that writers and artists in the West must confront; he would deal with these challenges at an intellectual level by the repudiation of Nietzsche. It should be noted that Gao had left China at the height of a Nietzsche craze in the Chinese intellectual world, and that hundreds of articles on the philosopher as well as new translations of his writings from the German were published in the 1980s. In the year or so prior to leaving China, Gao had read Hong Kong editions of all of Nietzsche's major works, and he felt a profound loathing for Nietzsche, particularly his notion of the Superman. From 1990, he would comment unfavorably on Nietzsche in eight essays, including his Nobel Lecture and his Nobel Centennial Lecture: "Bali suibi" 巴黎隨筆 (1991; tr. as "Parisian Notes," 2005), "Geren de shengyin" 個人的聲音 (1993; tr. as "The Voice of the Individual," 1995 and 2006), "Meiyou zhuyi" 沒有主義 (1993; tr. as "Without Isms," 1995–1996 and 2006), "*Meiyou zhuyi* zixu"《沒有主義》自序 (1995; tr. as "Author's Preface to *Without Isms*," 2006), "Wenxue de liyou" 文學的理由 (Nobel Lecture, 2000; tr. as "The Case for Literature," 2000), and "Wenxue de jianzheng: Dui zhenshi de zhuiqiu" 文學的見證：對真實的追求 (Nobel Centennial Lecture, 2001; tr. as "Literature as Testimony: The Search for Truth," 2001).

The two plays translated by Gilbert C. F. Fong in this present volume, Gao's *Escape* and *The Man who Questions Death*, are powerful indictments of Nietzsche's pernicious influence on the modern world. *Escape* is a scrutiny of the psychology of self-proclaimed heroes who, fired by self-righteous moral indignation for some cause (even those as noble as nation, democracy, and human rights), can lead others to sacrifice their lives for that cause; such causes become totems that can incite unthinking crowd behavior. There is no reference in the play to Nietzsche by name or any attempt to specifically equate such self-proclaimed heroes with Nietzsche's Supermen, but the inference is clear. The Nietzsche craze of the 1980s drew attention to the first Nietzsche craze in China that had occurred during the May Fourth era (1915–1921). It was then that China's modern literature was founded and youthful writers who were intoxicated by Nietzsche's writings believed that they were heroes whose writings would save China. Their "heroic" writings contributed to the spawning of patriotic heroes, particularly amongst young intellectuals, who willingly sacrificed their own critical thinking as individuals by capitulating to the dictates of politics. *The Man Who Questions Death* is a critique on the impact of Nietzsche's iconoclastic call for the revaluation of traditional values, for new authorities to overthrow old authorities. In Gao's analysis this had led to the introduction of a political dynamic for continuing revolution that had turned literature and art into the hostages of fashions and trends.

Significantly, both plays are unambiguously autobiographical, and in this respect they differ from the other sixteen plays of Gao's repertoire. For him his creations in art and fiction are solitary affairs, whereas his plays involve others: the cast, and all the specialists and stage technicians of the theater production. For the theater audience and for him, the playwright located in the audience, it is *theater*: entertainment. However, the autobiographical thrust of *Escape* and *The Man Who Questions Death* suggests a greater affinity with his autobiographical novels *Soul Mountain* and *One Man's Bible*, both of which were triggered off by Gao's trauma of watching his self being snuffed out by Mao Zedong's ideological manipulation of people's thinking, as well as the human tragedies he had witnessed in Mao's China. These were novels he had to write in order to expunge that trauma, and to celebrate and affirm the existence of his self.

In the plays *Escape* and *The Man Who Questions Death*, it was again personal trauma that induced him, the author, to take center stage as the protagonist to articulate his thoughts on issues that are of grave importance to him personally. Both plays are multidimensional, weaving issues that he has a compelling need to address as an intellectual, along the axis of events in his own life. Of significance is the fact that Gao is a master craftsman in expanding the expressive potential of language, and his innovative techniques succeed in Chinese as well as in English translation. Gao's brilliant dialogues, monologues and asides possess a luminosity that make his plays compelling reading as texts, as well as in stage productions. Wry humor and the absurd are not absent and, at a subliminal level serve to intensify the seriousness of issues addressed.

In the case of *Escape*, it was the trauma of witnessing events unfolding in Beijing on television news that resulted in his portraying of himself as Middle-Aged Man. In the case of *The Man Who Questions Death* it was the trauma of his confrontation with death in 1999 when he was hospitalized for one week because of bleeding in the stomach after he had taken the wrong medications. At the time he was spiritually and physically exhausted by the painful experience of revisiting the Cultural Revolution through writing *One Man's Bible*. Also, he was approaching sixty, and in the novel he mentions that he is not as agile as he once was, and that he had become a French citizen. It is highly likely that his sudden awareness of the inevitable depredations of the aging process on the physical self and the fact that he had totally broken his ties with China by becoming a French citizen may have compounded a sense of personal trauma that would project him into writing *The Man Who Questions Death*. In July 2000, when he came to Sydney, Australia, for the launch of *Soul Mountain*, he mentioned that he was in the process of writing this play in an interview with Phillip Adams in "Late Night Live" on ABC Radio National.

In the early months of 1989, a little over a year after Gao had settled in Paris, student activists in Beijing began cautiously to gather in Tiananmen Square to protest against bureaucratic corruption and to demand democracy. It was the seventieth anniversary of the May Fourth student demonstrations of 1919, and the tenth anniversary of the Democracy Wall movement of 1979, both of which had been brutally crushed by the authorities. However, in 1989, the authorities were embroiled in fierce power struggles at the highest echelons and were incapable of any decisive action against the students whose numbers began to swell with students from different provinces who had come to join in what they believed would be a historic moment in China's struggle for democracy. The continued inability of the authorities to act led to a growing optimism amongst the students that was both exhilarating and contagious. It seemed that victory was close at hand, and, while the students were waiting patiently for the authorities to accede to their demands, a festive, almost carnival atmosphere filled the Square. There was wild dancing to rock and heavy metal on ghetto blasters until army tanks rolled in with armed soldiers using live ammunition to evacuate the Square in the early hours of June 4, 1989.

These scenes appeared daily all over the world on televised news. Gao was outraged by the massacre of students in the Square and the large-scale beatings and arrests that followed. He voiced his anger at the actions of the Chinese authorities on French Television Channel 5 and in the Italian daily *La Stampa*: On both occasions he declared his resignation from the Chinese Communist Party. He applied for political asylum, and in September symbolically cut ties with China by sending to his publisher the manuscript of his novel *Soul Mountain* that he had begun writing in China in 1982. In late September of 1989 he started writing *Escape*, a play about the events in China, that he had agreed to write for an American theater company. He completed the play at the end of October but when the theater company requested revisions after reading the English translation, he withdrew the play and paid the translator, advising the theater company that while he was in China the Chinese Communist Party could not persuade him to revise his writings, and that he would not make any compromises for an American theater company. *Escape* was first published in 1990 in Stockholm in the first overseas issue of the Chinese-language magazine *Jintian* 今天, a reincarnation of the Beijing magazine of the same name that had been closed by the authorities a decade earlier during the Democracy Wall Movement.

The play opens with a male student and a woman broadcaster fleeing into a disused warehouse after tanks have rolled into an unidentified square that is unmistakably Tiananmen Square. It is close to daybreak when the authorities would begin to scour the vicinity to arrest anyone who had been in the Square. Both of them are traumatized by what they have just witnessed. The woman's clothes are splattered with the blood of the girl who was shot in the stomach as they were running alongside one another. She is close to being hysterical, but noticing something on the student's head, asks if he has been wounded. At that point he discovers that when the person running in front of him was shot in the head bits of the man's brains had splashed onto his head. Gripped by terror, the two instinctively cling to one another to confirm that they are still alive. Feelings of carnal lust arise, but they are interrupted by the arrival of a middle-aged man who has also sought refuge in the warehouse.

The three characters discuss the events that have just taken place in the Square from three perspectives, but all are aware that within a few hours they could be arrested and possibly executed. The student adopts a heroic stance and declares that despite the sacrifice of lives, the ultimate victory would belong to the students. The middle-aged man is cynical, and suggests that there should have been a retreat strategy, insinuating that it had been a dereliction of duty on the part of the student leaders that had led to the sacrifice of innocent lives. The student is incensed by the cynicism of the middle-aged man and, as time is running out, he decides to leave the warehouse and tells the other two to follow. However, as soon as he goes out of the door shots are heard, and then there is silence. The middle-aged man and the woman broadcaster assume that the student is dead, and they are assailed by the fear of death. At first life flashes before them, and they recall fragments of their past, but as daybreak fast approaches the hollow loneliness of impending death induces them to affirm life through the sexual reality of one another's bodies.

To censure the massacre is not the sole aim of the play. For Gao the existential state of mankind since ancient times has been an ongoing tragedy, and the play seeks to express modern man's predicament as a classical tragedy. In his instructions for the staging of the play he suggests that the performance should be imbued with the declamatory style of ancient Greek tragedy and the ritualized solemnity of ancient Chinese theater. The play is political, philosophical, and psychological, and should not be performed as a social–realist play reflecting only a single political event of the present. In "Guanyu *Taowang*" 關於逃亡 (1991; tr. as "About *Fleeing*," 2006; also tr. as "About *Escape*," 2007), Gao notes that his criticism of infantile features in the student movement had upset members of the Chinese democracy movement, and also that some writer friends regarded the play as being too political and not pure literature. While not a political activist, Gao defends his right to discuss politics in his writings. What he objects to are biased writings that "tie literature to the war chariot of a particular camp." He alludes to the thesis presented by Henri Laborit (1914–1995) in *Éloge de la fuite* [In praise of fleeing] (1976) that he read some time after writing the play: Once protest becomes organized, the protester's status is reduced to that of follower, and that the only escape is to flee. Laborit's thesis reinforced Gao's analysis of his own psychology and behavior during the Cultural Revolution, and he saw alarming similarities to that of the student protesters in Tiananmen Square. For him, life is constant fleeing, either from political oppression or from other people, as well as fleeing from one's self: "Once the self has awakened, what one finally cannot escape is this self, and it is this that is the tragedy of modern man."

Curiously, the play was reprinted in China in *On the Diaspora "Elite": Who They Are and What They Are Doing* (Beijing: China's Youth Publishing House, 1991) in May 1991. Preceding the full text of the play was a three-page article by Yu Sanniu (probably a pseudonym) attacking Gao Xingjian as a writer who was not in Beijing at the time for wrongly alleging that thousands of students had been killed in the Square. Much space is devoted to attacking the sexual promiscuity and moral depravity of the three characters in the play. According to Zeng Huiyan's article, "Publication of the Astonishing Book *On the Diaspora 'Elite': Who They Are and What They Are Doing*," in the Hong Kong bimonthly magazine *Baixing* 百姓 (no. 244, 1991), the book had been approved by the authorities for a print-run of 25,000 copies that had sold out after two months and had been reprinted.

The book provided examples of "reactionary" writings by "unpatriotic," "anti-Party" Chinese elites living abroad, and was eagerly read in China, but not with the effect intended by the authorities. The play premiered in Swedish in 1992 at the Kungliga Dramatiska Teatern in Stockholm and was followed soon after with performances at the Nürnberg Theater (1992; Nürnberg), Teatr polski (1994; Poznan), RA Theater Company (1994; Tours), Ryunokai Gekidan (1997; Osaka, Kobe, and Tokyo), Atelier Nomade (1998; Benin), and Haiyuza Gekidan (1998; Tokyo).

Over the following years Gao wrote a series of essays on aspects of literature in the context of China's modern intellectual history, and on specific problems that confronted Chinese writers. In 1996 these were published as a collection in *Without Isms*, and, as mentioned above, a number of these essays made reference to Nietzsche. In 1997 he began writing his autobiographical novel *One Man's Bible* in which he recalls his experiences during the Cultural Revolution, experiences that continued to haunt him in nightmares. Mao Zedong is portrayed as the embodiment of Nietzsche's Superman whose ego is bloated by his self-perception of his hero status as the savior of the nation, that he is in fact God. That Mao had been able to wreak havoc upon an entire population the size of China's was through his clever deployment of a multitude of lesser Supermen who also had bloated egos and saw themselves as heroes carrying out the sacrosanct bidding of the Great Leader.

In *The Man Who Questions Death* Gao mounts a powerful and sustained attack on Nietzsche and modernity. The play critiques contemporary art as the end of art, and also presents Gao's reflections on his own life and on the inevitability of death. The two actors dressed in black in fact present a soliloquy from two perspectives, in effect doubling the impact of the ideas expressed. This Man (a neurotic old man) and That Man (a somber older man) comment on the words and actions of one another; they observe each other closely but their eyes do not meet. Both actors refer to themselves as *you*, inviting the reader/audience to identify with them. This Man has missed his train and has to wait more than an hour for the next one, so he goes into a museum of contemporary art and is somehow locked inside. Surveying the exhibits of urinals, cigarette butts, used sanitary napkins, and so forth, he thinks that if it is possible for all this rubbish to be exhibited—undoubtedly with a catalogue containing critiques using the very latest jargon—then he as a living person, too, deserves to be one of the exhibits.

Amazed by his own genius for thinking of exhibiting himself as a live person, he notes that he will be world news, he would be like a soccer star without having had to do years of hard training and playing in matches. He admits to being narcissistic (just like everyone else) and is excited by the thought that he would be listed in art histories, become the subject of analysis, be subjected to repeated deconstruction, and win more acclaim than any of the other "artworks" on display. And he would become the topic of endless discussions by art critics. That Man speaks cynically as the voice of the inner mind of This Man.

Through the lips of the neurotic old man, Gao indicts Nietzsche's modernity as having set in motion the dynamic of needing to be sensational, to be seen as always doing something new, to be seen as a trendsetter, even if it is doing something puerile like masturbating in front of a camera. He regards this trend of continually subverting one's predecessors and debunking all old things as akin to a father teaching the son to shoot, and then the son killing the father so that he can be head of the family. Having pronounced the death of God, and afraid of being left behind, everyone charges forward wanting to be God. The neurotic old man then proceeds to voice his reflections on life, his desire not to be controlled, even by old age, even by death, and he decides to commit suicide right there and then.

Gao had first written the play in French as *Le Quêteur de la Mort*. Commissioned by the French Ministry of Culture, the script was read during Semaine de la SACD in the studio of Comédie Français in 2001. Ville de Marseille had proclaimed 2003 to be *L'Année Gao*, and, as one of the events, the play premiered at Théâtre du Gymnase in Marseille. In late 2002, while directing rehearsals in Taipei for his "modern" Peking Opera *Snow in August* Gao had collapsed and was hospitalized. He recovered sufficiently to direct the premiere performance in December before returning to Paris to direct the premiere performance of his play *Weekend Quartet* at Comédie Français. In February and March of 2003 he underwent major heart surgery; in June while directing rehearsals for *Le Quêteur de la Mort* he collapsed again, but was able to direct the premiere performance with the assistance of Romain Bonnin in September that year.

His failing health forced him to take stock of his life. He found that it was only possible for him to write poetry or paint, but only for a few hours each day. Nevertheless, several of his new paintings were hung at the Foire Internationale d'Art Contemporain (Paris, 2003 and 2004). He also had a number of solo exhibitions, notably those at Claude Bernard Galerie (Paris, 2004), Centra de Cultra Contemporainia (Barcelona, 2004), Frank Pages Art Galerie (Baden, 2005), and Singapore Art Museum (2005). By February 2005 he was strong enough to direct the staging of *Snow in August* at Opéra Marseille, and to receive his Honorary Doctorate from Taiwan National University at the International Gao Xingjian Symposium at Université de Provence that had been organized to coincide with the stage production of *Snow in August*.

By early 2006 his health had significantly improved. In February he has produced and submitted his "cinematic poem" *La Silhouette si non l'ombre* [Silhouette/Shadow] as an artistic film entry for the Cannes Film Festival; in March he traveled to Italy to attend two performances at the Venice Biennale of his play *Dialogue and Rebuttal* (in French, with the cast of the original French production); in April he attended the 24th Foire International de l'Art Contemporain in Brussels where Claude Bernard Galerie exhibited a large number of his new paintings and in November he attended the launch of his major solo exhibitions at Kunstmuseum Bern. During 2005 he also prepared four video lectures for the Faculty of Humanities of National Taiwan University. In these he addresses the following topics: "Zuojia de weizhi" 作家的位置 [The position of the writer], "Xiaoshuo de yishu" 小説的藝術 [Art in fiction], "Xiju de keneng" 戲劇的可能 [The possibilities in theater], and "Yishujia de meishu" 藝術家的美術 [The aesthetics of the artist].

List of Plates

Stage Performances of *Escape*

Plates 1 and 2

Premiere. Kungliga Dramatiska Teatern. Stockholm, Sweden. Directed by Björn Granath. 1992.

Plates 3 to 6

Nürnberg Theater. Nürnberg, Germany. Directed by Johannes Klett. Photographed by Marion Bühle. October 24, 1992.

Plates 7

Teatr polski. Poznan, Poland. Directed by Edward Wojtaszek. 1994.

Stage Performance of *The Man Who Questions Death*

Plates 8 to 15

Théâtre de Gymnase. Marseilles, France. Directed by Gao Xingjian and Romain Bonnin. September 23–26, 2003.

Plate 1

Plate 2

Plate 3

Plate 4

Plate 5

fluchtVERSUCHE
Absurd-komische Versuchsanordnung
zum dramatischen Leben und Werk von
Gao Xingjian 高行健

in vier Bildern:
Prolog
fluchtVERSUCH · grenzFLUCHT · theaterSUCHT · beziehungsSCHLUCHT
Epilog

Mitwirkende
Mann: Ulrich Voß
Frau: Tanja Thomsen
Gao: Matthias Faltz
Videomann/-frau: Peter René Lüdicke, Cui Yan
Musiker 1: Wu Wei
Musiker 2: Dietrich Petzold
Yin-Chor: Carolin Eichhorst, Sandra Klöss
Yang-Chor: Carsten Jenß, Christian Rodenberg

Stimmen vom Band:
Sandrine Adass
John Clark
Law Miu Lan
Wu Wei

Idee: Irmtraud Fessen-Henjes, Antje Budde
Regie/Collage: Antje Budde
Komposition: Dietrich Petzold, Wu Wei
Licht-/Rauminstallation: Andreas Schmid
Videoinstallation: Erhard Ertel
Ton/Licht/Tontechnik/Soundlayout: Philipp Richter
Öffentlichkeitsarbeit: Edith Krannich
Dramaturgieassistenz: Dagmar Paulus
Produktionsassistenz:
Elena Philipp, Law Miu Lan

gefördert durch:
der Hauptstadtkulturfonds der BRD

unterstützt durch:
Humboldt-Universitäts-Gesellschaft, e.V.
Seminar für Theaterwissenschaft
Kulturelle Kommunikation der
Humboldt-Universität zu Berlin
Institut für Theaterwissenschaft der Freien
Universität Berlin
Erhonders: GbR
www.kulturhilfegleitservice.de
sowie durch:
Frau Tilly Breitkreutz, Herr K. H. Trage
und weitere Sympathisanten

Impressum:
Herausgeber: théâtre DURAS
Premiere: 27.10.2001
Akademie der Künste, Berlin
Redaktion: Dagmar Paulus
Design: Carola Ludwig
Druck: Druckerei Schmohl&Partner
2,- DM

*Die Verwendung von Gao Xingjians Texten erfolgte
mit freundlicher Genehmigung des Autors.*

»Für mich gibt es keinen Zweifel. Ich gehe soweit, daß ich Zweifel an jeglicher Wertvorstellung hege. Nur am Leben zweifle ich nicht, weil das Selbst eine durchaus lebendige Existenz ist, [...] hat einen die Ethik transzendierenden Sinn. Wenn es für mich überhaupt noch einen Wert gibt, dann liegt er genau in der Existenz. Geistiger Selbstmord oder eher gesehen, bevor der natürliche Tod kommt, kann ich mir nur schwer vorstellen. Die Literatur ist für mich ein Mittel der Selbstrettung. Oder anders gesagt: Sie ist mir eine Lebensweise. Ich schreibe für mich und trachte nicht danach, andere zu vergnügen, [...] geht es mir nicht darum, die Welt oder andere Menschen zu verändern, denn ich, es ist unmöglich, lich, mich selbst zu verändern.«

Plate 6

Plate 7

Plate 8

Plate 9

Plate 10

Plate 11

Plate 12

Plate 13

Plate 14

Plate 15

Escape

逃亡

Characters

YOUNG MAN   20 years old

GIRL   22 to 23 years old

MIDDLE-AGED MAN   Over 40 years old

Time

From late night to early next morning

Location

An abandoned market in the city

Act I

[*The rumbling sound of tanks on tar road.*

In the near distance, the continuous crackling of machine guns and submachine guns.

An abandoned market in the city, which also looks like a rundown warehouse.

In a corner on left stage there is a small tin-plate door.

The door is pushed open, allowing a strand of pale white light to shine in from the streetlamp outside. YOUNG MAN, *panting and gasping for air, peeps in around the door and looks about intently at this strange place. A clutter of unidentifiable machinery and assorted objects are strewn all over the place.*

YOUNG MAN   *(To outside.)* Come on in! Quick!

GIRL   Anybody inside?

YOUNG MAN   Shh! *(Enters through the door.)*

[GIRL *comes in from outside the door, panting continuously.*

GIRL   So dark, can't see anything.

YOUNG MAN   You'll get used to it. *(Closes the door in a hurry.)* You're safe only when you can't see anybody.

[GIRL, *leaning against the door, takes a deep breath. Muffled crackling of machine guns.*

YOUNG MAN   They're still killing people out there!

GIRL	They actually opened fire on people! At first I thought they only shot rubber bullets into the air, but they used spotlights to track people down and actually shot at them!
YOUNG MAN	All dum dum bullets!
GIRL	What the …? Where did this blood come from? *(Sniffs her hands.)*
YOUNG MAN	Are you hurt?
GIRL	*(Feeling her body.)* All over, I've got blood all over me!
YOUNG MAN	Quick! Feel around and see if you can find the wound!
GIRL	My whole body, my … *(Weeps.)*
YOUNG MAN	Don't speak. They'll hear you outside!
GIRL	My whole body's … *(Goes limp.)*
YOUNG MAN	*(Feeling her clothes.)* Really? Where does it hurt? Tell me!
GIRL	My chest. I can't breathe. I'm going to die …
YOUNG MAN	Calm down! It's only on your dress. Other people's blood.
GIRL	I'm still alive?
YOUNG MAN	Of course you're alive.
GIRL	I don't want to be a cripple!
YOUNG MAN	Don't be silly. Here's your hands, and look, here's your arms. They're all there. You're perfectly all right.
GIRL	I saw her …

YOUNG MAN   Who did you see?

GIRL   I saw her, the girl running beside me. She was covering her stomach with her hands, she was about to open her mouth and cry out, but she didn't have time, she just collapsed onto her knees, and blood gushed out from between her fingers …

YOUNG MAN   There was a tank behind you at the time, smashing the roadblocks, the garbage cans, the bicycles and the tents to pieces.

GIRL   They were still inside, the people at the broadcasting station … I can't stand up any more …

YOUNG MAN   Straighten your legs, and your knees!

GIRL   They're burning …

YOUNG MAN   (*Feels her legs.*) They're fine, just a few scratches. Otherwise you couldn't have run that far.

GIRL   If you hadn't given me a hand and pulled me …

YOUNG MAN   You were suffering from shell shock. You almost got killed!

GIRL   (*Suddenly seizes* YOUNG MAN *in her arm.*) Tell me, am I still alive?

YOUNG MAN   Of course you're alive. We both are. We've managed to escape from the Square.

[*Sounds of machine gunfire coming from the near distance.*

GIRL   Oh! (*Holds him tight.*)

YOUNG MAN   They're clearing people out of the main streets.

GIRL	You think they'll come here?
YOUNG MAN	No, probably not for the time being. I think we're safe until daybreak.
GIRL	You've hurt your head!
YOUNG MAN	It's just some brain splatter. The guy was in front of me, and then I heard this pop, and the back of his head was blown right open … *(GIRL squats down.)* What happened to you?
GIRL	I've got it on my hands too. I feel sick … I'm going to puke …
YOUNG MAN	Well, what can we do about it? Just wipe it off on your clothes. They're covered in blood anyway.
GIRL	I can't stand the smell of blood.
YOUNG MAN	Take your dress off then. *(Walks away.)* Take your time and try to calm down a bit.
GIRL	Don't go.
YOUNG MAN	I'm right here beside you.
GIRL	Hold my hand.
YOUNG MAN	You're shaking.
GIRL	I really feel like crying.
YOUNG MAN	Cry then.
GIRL	I can't. But I really feel like crying out loud!
YOUNG MAN	Don't, they'll hear you outside. *(Holds her in his arms.)*

A

GIRL	I know. But I really feel like screaming. Just once, let me scream just once. And then I'll die, not seeing anything, not hearing anything … You hear that?
YOUNG MAN	Hear what? There's nothing there.
GIRL	Listen, listen!
YOUNG MAN	You're just being edgy.
GIRL	I can hear someone panting!
YOUNG MAN	You're panting.
GIRL	Someone's coming!

[*The door is pushed open, letting in a ray of light. Then it closes again.*

GIRL	A burglar?
YOUNG MAN	A burglar wouldn't risk his life and come out at a time like this. Maybe the guy escaped like we did. Ssh!

[*The door is pushed open in a hurry. The sound of fast-moving military vehicles on the street. The next moment, the shadow of a man is seen slipping in through the door in a flash. The door is closed instantly. Light from a cigarette lighter reveals a middle-aged man.*

YOUNG MAN	What do you want?
MIDDLE-AGED MAN	Just looking for a place to hide, to smoke a cigarette.
YOUNG MAN	You can't smoke in here.

MIDDLE-AGED MAN	The soldiers are setting fire to the whole city, and there's thick smoke everywhere. What do you care about one tiny little flame? Save your breath. It won't matter. Come over here and have a cigarette with me.
YOUNG MAN	*(Comes out of hiding.)* Did you escape from the square?
MIDDLE-AGED MAN	From my home. I can't even stay in my own home. *(Flicks the lighter on to see YOUNG MAN.)*
YOUNG MAN	They've already started searching door to door?
MIDDLE-AGED MAN	If you wait until they start searching, it'll be too late, won't it? *(Hands over a cigarette, lights the lighter, scrutinizes YOUNG MAN and sees that he is wearing a T-shirt.)* University student? What's happened in the Square?
YOUNG MAN	The place was surrounded by tanks. They turned on all the festival lights to shoot people. It was probably game over for those who didn't run. The roads were lined with bodies on my way here.
MIDDLE-AGED MAN	There are no more safe places in the city! Even if you stay in your own room, you can still be hit by a stray bullet flying in from outside. There was this old man living above me. He went out on the balcony to put his flowerpots away—He had a few pots of lilies in them, and he was afraid they'd be damaged by the smoke coming from the burning cars on the street. Who'd have thought that when he opened the balcony door, a bullet would hit him right between the eyes, and he'd die right there and then.

YOUNG MAN	Snipers, all specially trained. They were afraid to have their pictures taken. You know, they could be used as evidence of their crimes.
MIDDLE-AGED MAN	He was putting on a pair of glasses, he was very near-sighted. They say he was a retired accountant from the brewery or something.

[*Silence.*

MIDDLE-AGED MAN	(*Uses the light from his lighter to see.*) Is this a warehouse?
YOUNG MAN	Who knows what this place is.
MIDDLE-AGED MAN	(*Looks around.*) Is this a ladder, or a scaffold, or a gallows?
YOUNG MAN	Just like hell.
MIDDLE-AGED MAN	You can hide at the back in this place. Better than the slaughterhouse out there. It's all lit up. Were you the only one who managed to escape?

[GIRL, *who has already taken off her dress, hides hurriedly.*

YOUNG MAN	I ran with a group breaking away on the south side. They opened fire whenever they saw people running. We scattered and I got separated from the group, so I came in here. (*Blocks MIDDLE-AGED MAN.*) I figure it's safer inside. Why did you run?
MIDDLE-AGED MAN	Me? I got an anonymous phone call an hour ago, warning me that my life was in danger.
YOUNG MAN	Someone from the Public Security Bureau call you?

MIDDLE-AGED MAN	I think it was one of my friends in the know. That was his way of tipping me off to run for my life.
YOUNG MAN	You mean they've already got a blacklist of people they want to arrest?
MIDDLE-AGED MAN	They've got everything, from taped phone calls to videotapes of what happened in the Square. They also know who wrote which articles and who said what things. Everything's on their computers. They can arrest whoever they want. What can we do? We've only got one life to live, you know.
YOUNG MAN	What are we going to do? You think we can make it across the ring roads?
MIDDLE-AGED MAN	Who knows? The roads are lined with military vehicles. It all depends on how lucky you are. (*He chooses a place to sit down. Extinguishes the lighter and takes a deep sigh.*)
YOUNG MAN	So we'll just sit on our hands and wait?
MIDDLE-AGED MAN	There's still over an hour before it gets light.
	[*Silence. GIRL gets up from where she's hiding. She knocks something over.*
MIDDLE-AGED MAN	What's that? (*Immediately stubs out his cigarette.*)
	[*GIRL approaches the two men. MIDDLE-AGED MAN stands up and flicks on his lighter.*
YOUNG MAN	No! No lighter!
MIDDLE-AGED MAN	Oh, I'm sorry! (*Extinguishes lighter.*)

GIRL	*(To YOUNG MAN.)* What are we going to do?
MIDDLE-AGED MAN	You two really know how to enjoy yourselves, don't you? But it's the wrong time and the wrong place.
YOUNG MAN	Her clothes are all soaked in blood!
MIDDLE-AGED MAN	*(Cannot help getting agitated.)* What's a girl like you doing in a place like this?
GIRL	It was a bloodbath. They even did it to the old people and children, they were just bystanders! Bloodbath! You know what that means? At midnight there were crowds of people in the Square like it was a festival. No one could have expected something like that to happen.
MIDDLE-AGED MAN	They should have.
YOUNG MAN	And you?
MIDDLE-AGED MAN	They were worse than I'd expected.
YOUNG MAN	That's really something.
MIDDLE-AGED MAN	When you were mobilizing people you should have thought of ways to retreat.
YOUNG MAN	Did you?
MIDDLE-AGED MAN	I should have.
YOUNG MAN	Why didn't you get away sooner then? You wouldn't have to be in the mess you're in right now.
MIDDLE-AGED MAN	I was just curious to see how it would all end.

YOUNG MAN	You already knew the ending, did you? So why did you let yourself get drawn into it?
MIDDLE-AGED MAN	(*Laughs bitterly.*) I couldn't help it. I hated this sort of dirty politics right from the start. I'd had enough very early on.
YOUNG MAN	Who forced you?
MIDDLE-AGED MAN	Son, you don't have a monopoly on moral indignation. Everybody's entitled to it, otherwise there wouldn't have been so many people on the streets demonstrating and supporting you and your friends, and thousands of people wouldn't have had to be slaughtered!
YOUNG MAN	So do you think the people's struggle for democracy and freedom is totally meaningless?
MIDDLE-AGED MAN	(*At once getting agitated.*) Don't talk to me about "the people." They're just the millions of people living in this city, unarmed except for soft drink bottles and bricks. But bricks are no match for machine guns and tanks! It was so obvious. What they did was no more than a heroic way to committ suicide, but suicide just the same. People are so naïve, they can't help making fools of themselves.
YOUNG MAN	You included?
MIDDLE-AGED MAN	(*Bitterly.*) Yes.
YOUNG MAN	(*Pressing.*) Do you regret it?
MIDDLE-AGED MAN	(*Coldly.*) It's too late for regrets. I don't suppose you have any, do you, son?

YOUNG MAN	The people's struggle for freedom will triumph sooner or later, even if it has to be won with blood!
MIDDLE-AGED MAN	Why did you run away when the tanks rolled in?
YOUNG MAN	I didn't want to sacrifice myself mindlessly.
MIDDLE-AGED MAN	You didn't want to. Fine. But should I have sacrificed myself mindlessly then? Don't talk to me about "the people," or whether you're "the people" or I'm "the people." You're you, and you only, you don't even know whether you're able to understand or control yourself! And don't talk to me about the ultimate triumph. If freedom only results in death, then freedom is nothing more than suicide! When you've lost your life, what's the meaning of any final victory? The truth is: Both you and I have to run for our lives.
YOUNG MAN	But men aren't dogs …
GIRL	*(Stops YOUNG MAN.)* Never mind him. It'll be light soon!
YOUNG MAN	I can't stand his …
MIDDLE-AGED MAN	Son, you have to stand it even if you can't. You have to stand defeat. Your blind enthusiasm is futile in the face of death.
YOUNG MAN	Then turn yourself in. Do it now. Confess, tell them that you support the massacre, that they've only killed thugs and rioters, and that two of them are hiding here right now, and they've got bloodstains on them as well!
MIDDLE-AGED MAN	*(Smiles coldly.)* Maybe you could turn yourself in too. It's just as well. They'd rather let you go and not me.

They'd say that you're only a child, that you've been led astray, and that the people who started the riot were actually people like me. They've probably even got a confession ready, just waiting for a certain young man to read it out on television …

YOUNG MAN   That's an insult to my integrity!

MIDDLE-AGED MAN   They've insulted more than your integrity. They can easily crush your so-called "people" into minced meat, also in the name of "the people." So don't talk to me about "the people," and don't talk to me about "final victory" either. Escape! Escape is what we have to face now! It's destiny, yours and mine. *(Talks to himself.)* To live is to escape, to run for your life all the time!

[*The crackling of submachine guns close by.*

Silence. The three people stay close together. Scratching sound coming from the tin-plate door.

GIRL   *(Softly.)* Somebody's outside!

MIDDLE-AGED MAN   Block the door! *(Tiptoes forward and bars the door.)*

[*YOUNG MAN picks up a tool and holds it up high. He walks toward the door, his back against the wall. The scratching sound continues. It is piercing and becomes worrying.*

YOUNG MAN   *(Puts down the tool in his hand.)* Maybe it's someone else on the run?

MIDDLE-AGED MAN   Hold the door!

[*YOUNG MAN bars the door with the tool in his hands.*

Middle-aged Man, on all fours, listens with his ear to the ground.

YOUNG MAN — Shall we open the door?

MIDDLE-AGED MAN — Wait! He may have been followed!

[*Scratching sound continues. Girl closes her eyes.*

MIDDLE-AGED MAN — *(Gets up from the ground.)* He could be wounded.

YOUNG MAN — Shall we let him in?

MIDDLE-AGED MAN — Hold it. *(Holds his breath and listens intently with his eyes against the door. Scratching sound stops.)* He probably didn't make it. Open a crack and look first.

YOUNG MAN — *(Opens the door slightly.)* It's a dog.

MIDDLE-AGED MAN — A police dog!

GIRL — *(Screams in horror.)* Oh … *(Bites her finger.)*

[*Young Man immediately pushes the door closed. Silence.*

YOUNG MAN — I don't think so. A police dog would've barked already. Let me chase it away!

MIDDLE-AGED MAN — Leave it alone. There'll be trouble if it barks. The patrol'll be here in no time. Let's bolt the door!

[*The two move miscellaneous objects to block the door.*

GIRL — I can't take it any more….

YOUNG MAN	*(Goes to GIRL.)* It's nothing. Take it easy. Dogs get frightened by gunshots too. They'd run off in all directions. *(Comforts her.)*
MIDDLE-AGED MAN	*(Heaves a sigh of relief. Tries to find his cigarettes in his pocket.)* There's not much difference between men and dogs, except that men are a little bit smarter.

[YOUNG MAN *takes* GIRL *in his arms. As soon as* MIDDLE-AGED MAN *flicks on the lighter,* GIRL *immediately pushes* YOUNG MAN *away and covers her breast area with her hands.* MIDDLE-AGED MAN *turns to light his cigarette. The lighter flame is extinguished.*

GIRL	Men are more cruel than dogs.
MIDDLE-AGED MAN	*(Puffing smoke.)* People can't even save their own lives, let alone the lives of dogs.
GIRL	But when a dog tries to save people it has no regard for its own life.
MIDDLE-AGED MAN	Nicely said indeed. *(To YOUNG MAN.)* Are you sure you don't smoke?
YOUNG MAN	No thanks. Save the cigarettes for yourself.
MIDDLE-AGED MAN	*(Looks at his watch by the light of the cigarette.)* One hour to daybreak. I can't possibly smoke them all. *(Finds a place to lie down, then gets up again at once.)* This place is dark and damp. Careful you don't catch cold.

[YOUNG MAN *takes off his T- shirt to cover* GIRL.

GIRL	You're so nice. *(YOUNG MAN kisses her.)* Don't, don't. He'll see us.

YOUNG MAN	No one can see anything in here.
GIRL	But I can see the flicker of his cigarette. It worries me …
YOUNG MAN	Never mind him! *(Tries to kiss her.)*
GIRL	No, I can't … The cigarette …
YOUNG MAN	Hey you, can you put it out?
MIDDLE-AGED MAN	Then I won't be able to smoke them all. *(Counts the cigarettes in the dark.)* There are still one, two, three, four, five, six, seven, eight, nine, ten, eleven, twelve, thirteen, fourteen, fifteen, sixteen cigarettes. Ten minutes per cigarette on average…. Seven minutes, no, perhaps even five …
GIRL	I really can't take it any more!
YOUNG MAN	Close your eyes.
GIRL	I'm so nervous. There's a rumbling noise in my head …
YOUNG MAN	Just relax. Lean on me … *(Kisses her.)*
GIRL	I can't. My nerves are going to snap any minute!
YOUNG MAN	All your muscles are tense. You're really sensitive …
GIRL	I've got no feelings left, not even a little bit, my whole body's as stiff as a corpse. I wish somebody'd just shoot me and finish me off … I saw the horror in that girl's eyes, she wanted to scream, but before she could utter a sound, blood squirted out from between her fingers, it was all over her stomach … She fell onto her knees … I saw flames dancing in front of my eyes …

YOUNG MAN	Those were tracer bullets. They don't kill you. You can't see the bullets that kill people. They're too fast.
GIRL	But I saw fire and light ... so bright they dazzled me ... I nearly passed out ...
YOUNG MAN	Those were the spotlights round the Square ... They use them for dancing on the night of National Day ...
GIRL	It felt as if the lights were going right through me ... spilling all my guts out ...
YOUNG MAN	Don't be silly!
GIRL	Tell me, am I still in one piece? You've got to tell me!
YOUNG MAN	You're good, alive and well ...
GIRL	*(Going limp in his arms.)* This body of mine ... will it be able to squirm and move again? I want you to tell me!
YOUNG MAN	It's bloated, bound up really tight ...
GIRL	Please don't. Don't undo ... Oh ...
YOUNG MAN	Your whole body is talking ...
GIRL	Yes ...
YOUNG MAN	Don't cry ...
GIRL	Will I still be able to shed tears? To moan?
YOUNG MAN	You're shaking all over ... so alive ...
GIRL	No, I won't be able ... I won't ... I won't be able to do anything ... My head's going to explode ... I'm all covered in blood ... They're going to crush me to pieces ...

YOUNG MAN	Don't worry. I'm here … to caress you … so warm and soft …
GIRL	I don't know how long I can survive. I don't know if I'll still be alive the next moment. I'm afraid of daybreak.
YOUNG MAN	I'll protect you, I'll be with you all the time.
GIRL	You're so kind …
YOUNG MAN	It's fate. Fate has given you to me.
GIRL	I want to live, to live a good life, to be a good wife … a tender loving wife …
MIDDLE-AGED MAN	*(Stands up suddenly.)* Someone's coming! *(Puts out his cigarette.)*
GIRL	*(Her eyes are still closed.)* I can't hear anything. Where am I? Don't leave me, I'm dying … floating, floating on a river full of dead bodies …
YOUNG MAN	*(Pushes her away and shakes her.)* Wake up! Open your eyes!
	[*The sound of heavy footsteps approaching outside the door. All three are frozen into immobility. Silence. The sound of two or three people urinating on the ground. Footsteps recede.*
YOUNG MAN	Motherfuckers! *(Immediately takes* GIRL *in his arms and kisses her in a frenzy.)*
GIRL	*(She turns to avoid him and pushes him away. To* MIDDLE-AGED MAN.*)* Give me a cigarette. *(Hooks up her bra.)*
MIDDLE-AGED MAN	Sure. Can I flick on the lighter?

GIRL	*(Dryly.)* Yes.
	[MIDDLE-AGED MAN *lights her cigarette.* GIRL *takes a long puff and chokes.*
MIDDLE-AGED MAN	Don't inhale. Like this … *(Blows a smoke ring.)*
	[GIRL *imitates him. She throws her head back and exhales smoke.*
MIDDLE-AGED MAN	Ever smoked a cigarette before?
GIRL	Yes.
MIDDLE-AGED MAN	These aren't your trendy menthol cigarettes for girls. This stuff is for real.
GIRL	This is nothing. I've tried everything. *(Laughs neurotically.)*
MIDDLE-AGED MAN	Ever messed around with marijuana?
GIRL	Have you?
MIDDLE-AGED MAN	Yes, I have. I've tried everything, except that I've never smoked them while counting them one by one.
GIRL	Then just do it once for fun. You only live once, right? *(Again draws in a long puff and tries to blow a smoke ring.)*
YOUNG MAN	*(Moves forward, snatches her cigarette from her, and throws it away.)* That's enough!
GIRL	*(Taken aback.)* What do you think you're doing?
YOUNG MAN	*(Picks up the T-shirt.)* Cover yourself with this, okay?

GIRL	I won't bother! *(Pushes away the piece of clothing.)* It's dark in here. For all you know I could be wearing nothing. What the hell is it to you?
YOUNG MAN	*(Surprised.)* I ... I didn't mean to ... I was only worried that you might catch cold.
GIRL	*(Muttering to herself.)* You're not my husband. *(But still quietly takes the T-shirt and puts it on.)*
MIDDLE-AGED MAN	You've got a husband?
GIRL	*(Impatient.)* I've got a friend, a boyfriend! You could say he's my lover.
MIDDLE-AGED MAN	A lover's more interesting than a husband. Marriage is such a meaningless formality.
GIRL	But I still want to have a husband, to be a wife, at least once.
MIDDLE-AGED MAN	And then get a divorce?
GIRL	Why a divorce?
MIDDLE-AGED MAN	What I meant was, these days there are more divorces than marriages.
GIRL	If I got married it wouldn't be to get a divorce.
MIDDLE-AGED MAN	For what then?
GIRL	For love!
MIDDLE-AGED MAN	Of course.

GIRL	I also want to have his child.… He asked me to marry him once, but I didn't say yes.
MIDDLE-AGED MAN	Why not?
GIRL	I didn't want to have a child too early. Don't you think that I'm too young to be a mother? I want to spend a few more years acting, to be a good actress, you know, before I get married.
MIDDLE-AGED MAN	There doesn't seem to be any conflict there. You could get married first and then have kids a few years later.
GIRL	In show business, especially with actresses, if you get married before you've become famous …
MIDDLE-AGED MAN	Such a cruel profession. But girls still love to become actresses …
GIRL	It depends on what you've got.
MIDDLE-AGED MAN	You've got a good voice.
GIRL	You need more than a good voice.
MIDDLE-AGED MAN	Don't forget you also have a beautiful body. I happened to see it, accidentally.
GIRL	No need to explain. A beautiful body doesn't just look good to men but to women as well. But you can't become an actress with just a body.
MIDDLE-AGED MAN	Of course you've got to have special training, along with some talent. You appear to have both.
GIRL	I'm studying acting. That's my profession.

MIDDLE-AGED MAN	Are you a drama school student?
GIRL	I'm about to graduate. Quite a few theater companies and movie studios have talked to me already, but I haven't made up my mind yet.
MIDDLE-AGED MAN	I'm sure you'll be an excellent actress.
GIRL	*(Bitterly.)* Only if I can live through today.
MIDDLE-AGED MAN	There's no doubt about that.
GIRL	*(Heaves a sigh.)* Even if I manage to escape today, I can't become an actress now.
MIDDLE-AGED MAN	Why not?
GIRL	I was the girl on the radio, you know, the one who read all the antimartial law protests and declarations. I was on duty all day and all night inside the broadcast tent, just taking short naps when I could. I haven't had any real sleep for three days and three nights. I'm sure they must have recorded my voice already.
MIDDLE-AGED MAN	What a shame. Such a beautiful voice.
GIRL	Did you listen to the broadcasts?
MIDDLE-AGED MAN	More than once. I was excited by your passionate voice. So I said what I had to say, and then they accused me of incitement.

GIRL	You sure know how to talk. Did you draft those declarations too?
MIDDLE-AGED MAN	I couldn't get myself to write that sort of thing. Once in a while you'll see my name appearing on one of them. People came and asked me to sign. How could I say no?
YOUNG MAN	(*Deriding.*) Just couldn't help yourself, eh?
MIDDLE-AGED MAN	Exactly. Sometimes the signatures weren't even mine. People called you up and said your name had to be there. How could you refuse? Even though you knew very well that signing your name like that was suicidal, like a moth throwing itself into the fire.
YOUNG MAN	(*Curious.*) Are you a writer?
MIDDLE-AGED MAN	Well, how should I put it?
GIRL	You're afraid that I might turn you in once they've got me?
MIDDLE-AGED MAN	Girls don't usually do things like that.
GIRL	Stop saying "girl" this and "girl" that. We're all grown-ups here.
MIDDLE-AGED MAN	Excuse me. You're an actress, a very promising actress.
GIRL	Stop making fun of people all the time. You don't trust anybody!
MIDDLE-AGED MAN	(*Apologetic.*) That's true. It's not really one of my strong points.

GIRL	That's a common disease among you writers. You're used to criticizing people. You're sarcastic all the time. Can't you guys for once say something without any sting in it?
MIDDLE-AGED MAN	*(Trying hard to explain.)* I'm not that kind of critic. But I do get criticized by all sorts of people, so I have to be on the defensive all the time. *(Being honest.)* In fact, that's become a weakness of mine.
YOUNG MAN	Wonderful confession. *(Whistles once, then stops. Sits down. Silence.)*
GIRL	*(Sadly.)* They won't allow anyone to escape … I don't have any dreams left. I just wish I could be a wife, have a child and be a mother, at least once. I guess what I'm saying is, if a miracle should happen before you finish your pack of cigarettes.
MIDDLE-AGED MAN	You mean if we get lucky.
GIRL	Luck or miracle, what's the difference?
MIDDLE-AGED MAN	Miracles are gifts from Heaven, or they may appear as visions of God. But there is no God. As for luck, it's purely accidental. Life itself is an accident. We came into this world by accident when our parents made love; then we vanish, also by accident—war, disease, a massacre, a car crash, one way or the other.
YOUNG MAN	Can't you just shut up for a while? Let people calm down, will you?
MIDDLE-AGED MAN	See? She's already calmed down. You're the one that's all worked up.

YOUNG MAN   Your philosophy isn't worth a fart. It can't save anybody.

MIDDLE-AGED   And your rashness? Who can that save?
MAN

YOUNG MAN   Are you saying that we shouldn't have started the democracy movement?

MIDDLE-AGED   If a massacre is all it leads to, then it's better not to
MAN   have any.

YOUNG MAN   *(Stands up and approaches menacingly.)* What exactly do you mean by that?

MIDDLE-AGED   What I meant is: if you only care about starting
MAN   something without considering how it might end, and if you only go on the attack without organizing a retreat, then you shouldn't be in politics. You'll just become a sacrificial lamb in this game. You're really too green to be playing with politics, son.

YOUNG MAN   *(Irritated.)* I see, you've been around, you've got foresight. Why haven't I seen you stand up and be counted, and become a leader? Don't tell me you only know how to shoot your big mouth off!

MIDDLE-AGED   I've said it before, I was just a bystander, I was passing
MAN   through by accident, I became involved by accident, I got excited by accident, and I said a few words by accident, that's all there is to it. I've got my own things to do! Politics, I was sick and tired of it a long, long time ago. I'm not leadership material, and I don't have the itch for it. On top of that, we've got so many leaders already. I certainly don't want to get my hands dirty.

GIRL	Guys, stop arguing, will you? I've got a headache!
YOUNG MAN	Didn't you hear what he said? He's not one of us. He's only passing through!
GIRL	So what? Aren't we all running for our lives?
MIDDLE-AGED MAN	That's right. It's our destiny, yours, mine, even his. It's in a man's destiny to escape, to run for his life.
GIRL	The question is how? We can't just stay here and wait till we die.
YOUNG MAN	We've got to get out of here! We can't sit here and wait until daybreak. They'll come and take us away! We've got to cross the ring roads!
MIDDLE-AGED MAN	*(Coldly.)* Even dogs can't cross the ring roads, let alone humans.
GIRL	What do you think we should do?
MIDDLE-AGED MAN	Keep waiting.
GIRL	*(With bitterness.)* Wait for lady luck to come?
MIDDLE-AGED MAN	*(Calmly.)* We'll wait until just before daybreak when the streetlights are turned off, and see if there's any chance of crossing the ring roads in the dark. In the morning, there'll be pedestrians. They'll have to let things get back to normal, right? Workers'll have to go to work and the farmers'll have to go into the city to sell their vegetables. Maybe we could blend in with the crowds going in and out of the city.
YOUNG MAN	You think there'll still be people going to work on a day like this?

MIDDLE-AGED MAN	People will do anything with a gun pointed at them. They'll still have to go to work as usual, do business, repair shoes, drive cars, make money to buy food. People are such cowards.
YOUNG MAN	But the entire city is fighting against the massacre! Workers will go on strike for sure, and the struggle will get more ferocious. *(To GIRL.)* We have to tell the truth about the massacre as soon as possible, spread the protest to the whole nation, and call for a general strike by the workers and students! A civil war will soon break out!
MIDDLE-AGED MAN	A civil war? Stop kidding yourself. You got any weapons?
YOUNG MAN	We've had word that the army's already split into factions.
MIDDLE-AGED MAN	And you're pinning your hopes on that? On the wheeling and dealing between the army and the politicians? Haven't you had enough of their playing the student protest card, using students like you?
YOUNG MAN	Aren't you a card too? And a small one at that!
MIDDLE-AGED MAN	You're right about that. Just because I don't want to be a playing card in someone else's hand, I've got to have my own will, my own independent and immovable will. So I've no choice but to run away!
YOUNG MAN	*(Becomes calm and hostile.)* I see. Then are you running away from us as well? Running away from the democracy movement?

MIDDLE-AGED MAN	I run away from everything related to the so-called collective will.
YOUNG MAN	If everyone were like you, there'd be no hope for this country.
MIDDLE-AGED MAN	What's a country? Whose country? Has it taken any responsibility for you and me? Why should I be held responsible for it? I'm only responsible for myself.
YOUNG MAN	And you'd just watch and let our nation perish?
MIDDLE-AGED MAN	I'm only interested in saving myself. If one day our nation is going to perish, then it deserves to perish! This is exactly what you want to hear from me, right? Any more questions? Is the inquisition over?
YOUNG MAN	*(Puzzled.)* You're a …
MIDDLE-AGED MAN	An individualist? A nihilist? Let me tell you, I don't subscribe to any ism, I don't need to. I'm a living human being. I'm not going to put up with being massacred, or being dragged away and forced to kill myself.
YOUNG MAN	*(To GIRL.)* We shouldn't stay here with him any more. Let's go!
GIRL	*(To MIDDLE-AGED MAN.)* What do you think you're doing? *(To YOUNG MAN.)* Don't go!
YOUNG MAN	I'll go by myself then! *(Walks toward the door.)*
MIDDLE-AGED MAN	Stay or go, that's for us to decide for ourselves.
GIRL	*(Holds YOUNG MAN. To MIDDLE-AGED MAN.)* You're going to let him go like that? He'll get himself killed.

MIDDLE-AGED MAN	I just want to make him understand that a man is nothing standing in front of a tank or a machine gun.
YOUNG MAN	*(Hollers.)* You think we haven't confronted tanks?
MIDDLE-AGED MAN	But that was before they decided to shoot at the people, before they mapped out their plans, before they finished negotiating the deals among themselves.
YOUNG MAN	All that bloodshed for nothing? But history, history will remember this day! This blood-stained day! *(Shouts.)* This victorious day—
GIRL	*(Grabs YOUNG MAN.)* Don't shout!
	[*Silence. YOUNG MAN tries to suppress his sobbing.*
MIDDLE-AGED MAN	*(Talks to himself.)* History? Who's going to write it? You? Me? Or they? History is a piece of dirt, a pile of useless waste paper.
GIRL	You're so cold! *(Suddenly explodes.)* Shut the hell up! *(Softly to YOUNG MAN.)* What's come over you?
YOUNG MAN	Leave me alone.
GIRL	He's crying.
MIDDLE-AGED MAN	*(Goes over to YOUNG MAN.)* Son, let me salute you. I just don't want to be your tail.
YOUNG MAN	You make me sick.
MIDDLE-AGED MAN	I know. I make everybody sick. *(Sits down and takes out a cigarette. He puts it in his mouth and flicks on his lighter.)*
GIRL	Your heart is dead.

MIDDLE-AGED MAN	*(Taken aback.)* Perhaps.

[*Silence.* MIDDLE-AGED *MAN extinguishes the lighter. Lowers his head.*

GIRL	How many more cigarettes?
MIDDLE-AGED MAN	Thirteen, maybe twelve. Who knows? You want one?
GIRL	No thanks. *(Notices that* MIDDLE-AGED MAN *is not smoking.)* Why aren't you smoking?
MIDDLE-AGED MAN	I'm trying to quit.
GIRL	You tried that many times?
MIDDLE-AGED MAN	Yes.
GIRL	You can't change what you are.
MIDDLE-AGED MAN	People are like that.
GIRL	Don't keeping talking about people. Are you a philosopher?
MIDDLE-AGED MAN	No, fortunately.
GIRL	I can't stand men talking about philosophy.
MIDDLE-AGED MAN	Then what shall we talk about?
GIRL	Anything. *(Stops.).*You live close by?

MIDDLE-AGED MAN	Not far from the flyover.
GIRL	Once you came out, you couldn't go back?
MIDDLE-AGED MAN	My wife urged me to make a run for it. She answered the phone. At once her face went as white as a sheet. I told her briefly what to do before I left in a hurry. Our kid was already asleep.
GIRL	Boy or girl?
MIDDLE-AGED MAN	A little girl. She was crying all night, so I made a bed on the floor for her to sleep on. Stray bullets, you know. She was tired too. As soon as she fell asleep the phone rang.
GIRL	You have a happy family. Your wife is really nice to you. Why did you say that you're against marriage?
MIDDLE-AGED MAN	Look at you two. You're happy, aren't you? You escaped together, sharing each other's hardships. That's what I'd call romantic.
GIRL	I wouldn't run away if I had a home like yours.
MIDDLE-AGED MAN	I was afraid they'd take me away in front of my little girl.
	[*Silence.*
GIRL	If they arrested me, I'd rather die.
MIDDLE-AGED MAN	There's no need.
GIRL	I'm afraid of being punished. I can't stand torture. I have a low pain threshold.

MIDDLE-AGED MAN	(*Sighs.*) You're right, they're capable of anything.
GIRL	Let's not talk about this!
MIDDLE-AGED MAN	About what then?
GIRL	I don't know.
	[*Silence.*
MIDDLE-AGED MAN	You two could get married right now.
GIRL	(*Laughs nervously.*) You must be kidding.
MIDDLE-AGED MAN	I'm serious.
GIRL	(*Softly.*) We've only just met.
MIDDLE-AGED MAN	He's not your boyfriend?
GIRL	I don't even know his name.
MIDDLE-AGED MAN	(*Surprised.*) Well, a name is only a sign. He's a nice young man.
GIRL	We ran away from the Square together. I was shaken, I couldn't move. He helped me along and then I ran behind him …
MIDDLE-AGED MAN	Anything's possible. Life is full of accidents. You'll be safe with him. He has a strong sense of responsibility.
GIRL	He saved my life. (*Suddenly starts to sob.*)

MIDDLE-AGED MAN	*(Gets up and walks away. He steps in a puddle of water.)* Where did this water come from? *(Flicks on his lighter and notices a puddle of water beneath his feet.)* Where's the leak?
YOUNG MAN	*(Comes over to have a look.)* It didn't seem to be there when we first came in.
GIRL	Maybe someone didn't turn the tap off properly? Let's go find the tap. *(Gets excited and hurriedly goes to get her dress.)*
MIDDLE-AGED MAN	*(Lights up the source of the water with his lighter.)* It looks like the water's coming in from outside …
YOUNG MAN	Maybe they broke a water pipe at a construction site somewhere around here?
MIDDLE-AGED MAN	Who knows?
GIRL	*(Squats down by the puddle and washes her dress. Smells it.)* Yuck! Smells like mud! *(Gets up. Throws the dress away.)*
YOUNG MAN	Maybe the water seeped in from an underground sewer. *(Climbs up the scaffold and looks down rather childishly.)* The place'll soon be flooded and turn into a swamp!
GIRL	It'd be good if it really became a swamp. Then nobody'd be able to come in here.
MIDDLE-AGED MAN	*(Watches by the side of the puddle.)* The water's flowing very slowly, as if it's not really moving. It's probably been like this for a while. *(Looks down intently with the light from his lighter.)*

GIRL	What are you looking at?
MIDDLE-AGED MAN	A mirror.
GIRL	Pardon me?
MIDDLE-AGED MAN	Right now it's calm and smooth, just like a mirror. You can see yourself in it. And it looks so deep and so serene …
	[*GIRL can't resist coming over and looks down at her own reflection in the water. She turns in a circle unwittingly.*
MIDDLE-AGED MAN	Don't you think she looks wonderful? (*Holds up the lighter close to her to light up her face.*)
	[*The two look down attentively. GIRL touches the puddle of water with her toes and turns away.*
MIDDLE-AGED MAN	Why did you break it?
GIRL	(*Closes her eyes.*) It's only a puddle of dirty water. 死水
MIDDLE-AGED MAN	You can't really be sure which is more real, the dirty water or the reflection. The simplest things are always the hardest to understand. For instance, can you be sure … What's happened to you?
	[*Holds up his light and turns to light up her face.*
GIRL	Nothing.
YOUNG MAN	He's playing a game with you.
GIRL	(*Suddenly inspired, playfully.*) Why not? A game before dying. (*She just takes the lighter from MIDDLE-AGED MAN*

and holds it up high.) I'm holding a torch in my hand, I'm the Goddess of Freedom! I'm your idol. *(Giggles, then talks to herself.)* But I can't overcome my own troubles. I walk on the edge of an abyss, I look at the deep and secret water, which reminds me of the skipping elastic I used to jump over when I was small. *(To YOUNG MAN.)* How do you sing that song? *(Talks to herself.)* It's always in my head, but I've forgotten … *(Loudly.)* I'm the Goddess of Life. With a torch in my hand, I'm walking on a bridge, a single-plank bridge. I stare at the abyss below my feet, I don't know if I'll get across safely …

MIDDLE-AGED MAN	*(Softly.)* Give it a try.
GIRL	But I'm afraid, afraid of this dark and secret water.
MIDDLE-AGED MAN	It's only a puddle of dirty water—
GIRL	No, it's deep, it's bottomless. It'll engulf me.
MIDDLE-AGED MAN	Just try it once, for good or for ill.
GIRL	No, this is no fun. Can't you think of something more interesting? *(To YOUNG MAN.)* Come over here. Let's play together!
YOUNG MAN	I'm no actor.
GIRL	It's so tiring being with you.
YOUNG MAN	Find someone not tiring then.

GIRL	*(To YOUNG MAN.)* Come, dance with me! Do you remember? Those midnight and small-hour gatherings, the concerts of ten thousand at the feet of the Goddess of Freedom. All around were loudspeakers blaring out the curfew order. We didn't have anything, just jumping, rocking and rolling in the Square, feverishly rocking and rolling! Come! Come over here and dance with me!
YOUNG MAN	*(Gets down from the scaffold and reluctantly dances a few steps. Stops.)* There's no music.
GIRL	The music's in our hearts! Let's sing silently and dance—
YOUNG MAN	I can't go on. Ask him to dance with you. *(Turns his back on GIRL.)*
GIRL	So quiet. As if nothing'd happened. Nothing, there's nothing. What's come over you two? Let me tell you, at a dance I wouldn't dance with anybody even if they asked me.
MIDDLE-AGED MAN	*(Walks over to GIRL.)* I'll dance a number with you. But I can't keep up with your fancy new steps.
GIRL	Let's try an old-fashioned dance then. *(Smiles softly.)*
MIDDLE-AGED MAN	Cheek-to-cheek?
	[The lighter is extinguished. MIDDLE-AGED MAN holds GIRL in his arms. The two of them are not dancing, only standing silently cheek-to-cheek.
GIRL	*(Softly.)* Tell me, do you love your wife?

MIDDLE-AGED MAN	I used to.
GIRL	Have you loved any other women?
MIDDLE-AGED MAN	What do you think? *(Gently caresses her.)*
YOUNG MAN	*(Walks past MIDDLE-AGED MAN.)* Ladykiller!
GIRL	What did he say?
MIDDLE-AGED MAN	He said you're very lovely.
GIRL	Sounds like something you'd have said.
MIDDLE-AGED MAN	Why ask if you heard it?
GIRL	Just wanted to be sure.
MIDDLE-AGED MAN	It's not enough to feel it?
GIRL	I like voices in the dark. There's a kind of mystery in them.
MIDDLE-AGED MAN	Women have more mystery.
GIRL	I thought you already knew everything.
MIDDLE-AGED MAN	But I haven't lived my life to the full. *(About to kiss GIRL. She pushes him away.)*
GIRL	*(Walks to one side and closes her eyes.)* I see big chunks of snow falling, big chunks, big chunks …

YOUNG MAN	*(Sits on the scaffold. Childishly and mischievously.)* Leaflets, leaflets, big bundles of leaflets, curfew orders dropping from helicopters!
GIRL	Don't interrupt!
YOUNG MAN	You can talk, so can I.
GIRL	I want to put on a show!
YOUNG MAN	Put on anything you want. People are free not to watch.
GIRL	*(Shouts at him.)* You let me perform! I want to act! Act! *(Silence. She covers her face with her hands and sobs quietly.)*
MIDDLE-AGED MAN	*(Walks over to her side, softly.)* He was just being childish. Never mind him. *(Prompting her.)* Big chunks of snow are falling … Good, go on.
GIRL	I see big chunks of snow falling, crushing the entire Square and all the streets, like a big shroud covering the city—
YOUNG MAN	*(Loudly.)* I saw a black sun, its pallid deathly light shining on the people in mourning clothes—
GIRL	*(Insistently.)* I see big chunks of snow falling, the city is a big patch of white. Big chunks of snow, falling silently, without a sound …
YOUNG MAN	They're all standing to attention in the Square, now clean and white, taking part in a requiem for the dead, in memory of the countless people who sacrificed their lives in the bloodbath …
GIRL	The world is a huge patch of white. We climb up onto the crumbling city wall, it's overgrown with weeds. The air is cold but crisp. Big chunks of snow are falling …

YOUNG MAN	I want to rise up from the blood, I want to live on, live to see that day when it comes!
GIRL	You're holding my hand, together we climb up the crumbling city wall. The streets are covered with snow, cars and pedestrians, they're moving slowly, they've become very small. We're walking on top of the city wall, you're holding my hand … (*MIDDLE-AGED MAN gingerly holds GIRL's hand.*) We exhale puffs of hot breath. The cold, fresh and crisp, stings our cheeks, but it's a pleasurable sensation. I watch as chunks of snow continue to fall. The sound of the city has become faint and distant. The air feels like it's been filtered. You exhale puffs of white breath, you pull down my little felt hat to cover my ears. My fingers are all red and frozen, there's no feeling in them. It's you, you're holding my hand, you're exhaling puffs of white breath …
YOUNG MAN	We'll live to see the day, we'll live to see the day …
GIRL	(*Ignores MIDDLE-AGED MAN's hand which is holding her.*) But I won't be there …
YOUNG MAN	No, we'll have to live, to break away from this darkness. I dream of that day, the day of national mourning, we'll have a big ceremony.
MIDDLE-AGED MAN	(*Recoils. A little bit sad. Talks to himself.*) I'll slip away quietly …
GIRL	(*Walks away by herself. Talks to herself.*) No, I want to dress up and make a beautiful entrance at the festival party. (*Walks in front of the puddle of water, flicks on the lighter and holds it with both hands.*) I want to look at my body in the mirror …

YOUNG MAN   A nation full of sorrow … in grief and in pain …

MIDDLE-AGED   *(Stares at the light in* GIRL'*s hand.)* I feel sorry for
MAN   myself … In my heart there's just this secret light, you
               try to protect this secret light, but it's as if you're
               walking on the river of death and a ghostly wind is
               blowing from all sides, and the light'll go out at any
               moment …

GIRL   I want to have a mirror as big as a wall, to look at myself,
               to look at the big chunks of falling snow. I walk on the
               snow, completely naked, my body and soul are so
               clean and clear, as though I've just finished making
               passionate love with him, and I've forgotten myself …

YOUNG MAN   I sit by the seashore, the waves come crashing in. I look
               at the endless grayish sea, the mountainous breakers
               leaping and tossing about. Under the pallid sky, a line
               of sea spray soars up into the air above the shadowy
               swells …

MIDDLE-AGED   You walk on the shady river of death, guarding the last
MAN   sliver of light in your heart. This vision, I always see
               this vision, it haunts my dreams. I can't even tell if it's
               a dream or an illusion, or just a feeling …

GIRL   I hold a candle in my hand, do you remember? At the
               New Year party I have on a white dress, like a little
               girl, I walk in a dignified procession on a single-plank
               bridge, the dark and secret water flowing beneath
               my feet. We're playing a game, I'm skipping over the
               elastic. Do you still remember that song? How does
               it go? Let's all skip together—

               [*The lighter is extinguished.*

YOUNG MAN GIRL	On a deserted beach, only you and I are there, two naked bodies …
	How come I can't remember how the song begins? All of us girls sing that song, it's a very familiar song, how could I have forgotten? We're playing in the small alley in front of our house. You boys are such a nuisance. You keep crossing over our elastic skipping rope on purpose.
YOUNG MAN	We're rolling around on the sand, like two mischievous children …
GIRL	You boys are all very bad; you're very bad then as well. You tell me to go into the small room, saying you want to show me a picture book, but what kind of book is it! Where did you get a dirty book like that? You've got something really bad on your mind!
MIDDLE-AGED MAN	You're always walking in swamps that are neither deep nor shallow. Your hands, your feet, and your body are all wet. It's very uncomfortable, and you always want to find a dry spot to …
GIRL	It's a very hot summer. At night everyone sits in the yard cooling off. You and I come out of the small room, and people stare at us strangely. I deliberately hold my head high, but I'm not that pure any more. I want to tell you, I'm not that pure—
MIDDLE-AGED MAN	You always get tangled in waterweeds. I've had this dream for many years. The dark and secret deathly water, under your feet is nothing but waterweeds, you can't get out of the swamp no matter how hard you try …

GIRL	He's very rough …
YOUNG MAN	I just sit on the shore, staring at the end of this stretch of deathly water and the gray sky connected to the clouds. I keep staring, staring at the stretch of sky …
GIRL	Ants are crawling inside my body. They're crawling backward and forward over my body, they're crawling out of my ears and my nostrils, they're eating me. In Africa there's a type of huge man-eating ant. I used to be very afraid of them, but I'm not afraid any more, I'm happy to let them crawl backward and forward over my body …
YOUNG MAN	My mother, pretty soon she'll be old …
GIRL	I want to hear him speaking in my ear … under the soft downy sheets … being close to his body …
MIDDLE-AGED MAN	Swamp … wet and soggy … still walking …
YOUNG MAN	(*Suddenly sits up.*) It's smashed!
MIDDLE-AGED MAN	What's smashed?
GIRL	The fish tank's smashed.
YOUNG MAN	What fish tank?
GIRL	The fish tank on the windowsill. I'd forgotten to close the window. There was a gust of wind. It blew the curtain open and it hit the fish tank and smashed it. The goldfish are struggling on the floor, they're struggling for their lives …

死 水

YOUNG MAN	I meant it was my head that was smashed. I had a bad dream. They shot a bullet into my head, and it went bang and was smashed!
GIRL	*(Rushes over to him.)* Don't try to scare me, you and your endless talk about smashed heads! It's so annoying! I've had enough of your stories about heads. I was talking about a fish tank, the one I bought for my father. I was an intern at the studio and they took some shots of me. That was the first time I made any money on my own, so I bought my father a fish tank.
MIDDLE-AGED MAN	*(Teasing GIRL.)* I wouldn't mind having a daughter like you.
GIRL	You don't deserve one.
	[*Silence.*
YOUNG MAN	Hey, what time is it?
GIRL	No light. Don't flick the lighter on.
MIDDLE-AGED MAN	You forget you've got the lighter in your hand.
GIRL	Let's stay in the dark. Never mind what time it is.
MIDDLE-AGED MAN	Just mumbling in the dark?
GIRL	Just submerge ourselves in our own minds.
YOUNG MAN	We've all become the living dead, like in hell!
GIRL	It'd be good if it were really like this.

MIDDLE-AGED MAN	*(Listening intently.)* It's so quiet. No more gunshots. A dead city, a ruin, all deserted …
YOUNG MAN	*(Jumps down from scaffold.)* No, I've got to get out. *(Starts to remove the objects blocking the door.)*
GIRL	What are you doing?
YOUNG MAN	I've got to go out and have a look. I can't die in here waiting.
GIRL	Have you gone crazy?
YOUNG MAN	We can't die cooped up in here. We've got to break out of here!
GIRL	They'll shoot you!
YOUNG MAN	Don't take me for a fool. I'll go out and take a look first.
GIRL	But you won't be able to come back. *(To MIDDLE-AGED MAN)* Say something!
MIDDLE-AGED MAN	Maybe he's right. Give me the lighter. *(Takes the lighter, flicks it on and looks at his watch.)* The streetlights are probably out. *(Helps to remove the objects blocking the door. Listens with his eye to the door.)*
YOUNG MAN	Anything?
MIDDLE-AGED MAN	No cars, and no footsteps.
GIRL	They're gone!
MIDDLE-AGED MAN	They've finished. It's all over.
YOUNG MAN	I'll open the door!

MIDDLE-AGED MAN	Wait. Let's discuss how we're going to get out. The target'll be too big if all three of us go at the same time.
YOUNG MAN	I'll go first. *(To GIRL.)* You follow me.
GIRL	If they open fire, we won't be able to come back.
	[*Silence.*
YOUNG MAN	Then we won't.
MIDDLE-AGED MAN	They're not a bunch of stupid sheep. They're using submachine guns. We've got to spread out and cross the road from three different places. Then we'll join up again.
YOUNG MAN	You go your way and we'll go ours.
GIRL	My heart's pounding like crazy … I've got a bad feeling …
YOUNG MAN	Okay then. I'll go first. You wait here. If it's clear, you come after me. *(Opens the door a little bit.)* The streetlights are out. Quick! *(Dashes out of the door.)*
MIDDLE-AGED MAN	Wait! *(Keeps GIRL down.)* Wait until I've gone out. *(A gunshot is clearly heard as he is about to go out of the door. He closes the door immediately.)*
GIRL	*(Screams.)* They've killed him!
MIDDLE-AGED MAN	Don't shout! *(Covers GIRL's mouth.)*
GIRL	They've killed him! Let me go!
MIDDLE-AGED MAN	They'll hear you!

GIRL	*(Storms the door in an attempt to get out.* MIDDLE-AGED MAN *stops her and holds her in his arms.)* You let me out of here—
MIDDLE-AGED MAN	Are you nuts?
GIRL	*(Sobbing.)* They've murdered him … Why did you let him leave? Let me go! You're so selfish … you bastard! *(Beats* MIDDLE-AGED MAN *in a frenzy.)*
MIDDLE-AGED MAN	*(Crestfallen, he releases her and lets her hit him.)* I didn't think … I guess I should have …

[GIRL *jumps on him and tries desperately to restrain herself, gasping continuously.* MIDDLE-AGED MAN *caresses and comforts her, combing her hair.*

MIDDLE-AGED MAN	They'll be here any minute now. Let them come.
GIRL	Let them take me. Let them beat me to death!
MIDDLE-AGED MAN	Don't be silly. You're still young. They'll release you some day. You've got to live until the day, *(Bitterly.)* the day of victory for freedom.
GIRL	I'll be very old then, tortured out of shape … I don't want to live till that day! I don't want to live!
MIDDLE-AGED MAN	*(Irritated.)* Stop being hysterical! *(Slaps her in the face.)*

[GIRL *is stunned. She looks at* MIDDLE-AGED MAN *in a stupor.*

MIDDLE-AGED MAN	*(Harshly.)* Go to the back and wait! Don't shout if they come looking for us. Don't utter a sound! *(GIRL is not moving.)* Go and hide at the back, didn't you hear me?

GIRL	*(Pitifully and softly.)* Don't leave me on my own …
MIDDLE-AGED MAN	I'm not going to go out and get myself killed. I'll just wait here, smoking my cigarettes.
GIRL	*(Grabs MIDDLE-AGED MAN's hand.)* Don't smoke. I'm scared of fire and light, I'm scared of everything …
	[*MIDDLE-AGED MAN holds her in silence and kisses her. She stands on her toes, enraptured.*
MIDDLE-AGED MAN	*(Pitying her, softly.)* It's okay. Be a good girl. Go to the back and wait.
GIRL	*(Muttering.)* No, I like it this way … I'm not …
MIDDLE-AGED MAN	No! I can't … silly girl …
GIRL	You're being silly! Quick …
MIDDLE-AGED MAN	I haven't got the urge … I can't make love at gunpoint!
GIRL	*(Kisses him madly.)* They could be here any minute … I don't know if I can live through this moment … I hope this will end soon … *(Protesting.)* What are you waiting for?
MIDDLE-AGED MAN	Really, I can't … *(Moved, very gently.)* You're such a nice girl—
GIRL	I'm a woman!
MIDDLE-AGED MAN	Yes,… a real woman …
GIRL	A good woman …

Middle-aged Man	Very much like a woman ... sensitive ...
Girl	Wild ...
Middle-aged Man	Wanton ...
Girl	Clear—Oh—

[*In the dark there comes the sound of flowing water. The dark puddle of water gradually spreads and extends.*]

Act II

[*A faint gleam of morning sun filters through from above the stage; it is sometimes light and sometimes dim. The surrounding walls and objects are almost invisible in the dusk, making the scene appear stranger than it already is, like the inside of a building drowned in water or a stretch of swamp.*

MIDDLE-AGED MAN and GIRL are naked, lying on a wooden structure on top of the water.

GIRL	A boat.
MIDDLE-AGED MAN	What?
GIRL	A sailboat, drifting on the water, don't know where it's drifting to. Don't know whether I'm dead or alive …
MIDDLE-AGED MAN	No distinction between you and me. No presence, and no absence. A great mass of emptiness and chaos …
GIRL	Can't see any stars or lights. Where am I? Only a few strange shadows …
MIDDLE-AGED MAN	Unfathomable, incomprehensible, no thoughts, no desires …
GIRL	A flickering cigarette flame, a one-handed caress, too lazy to move, dreaming, yet so awake, a dream which is real …

MIDDLE-AGED MAN	The marches, gatherings, protests, and quarrels, the moral indignation, the declarations, the soft drink bottles, the squashed cardboard boxes, the garbage on the Square, they're no more, all gone. It's unimaginable: never been so relaxed, no desire to do anything, no need to hurry any more.
GIRL	No exams, no dates, no need to rush to see a disappointing movie, no more harrowing looks, no more memories, no more regrets.
MIDDLE-AGED MAN	Two bodies without a soul.
GIRL	Only giddiness and exhaustion.
MIDDLE-AGED MAN	You were insatiable …
GIRL	You were wild …
MIDDLE-AGED MAN	In the face of death, hopes and desires become nothing more than illusions.
GIRL	*(Opens her eyes.)* Where's this light coming from?
MIDDLE-AGED MAN	*(Also opens his eyes.)* Oh, it's already morning. *(Sits up.)* The sun hasn't come up yet.
GIRL	They've forgotten us.
MIDDLE-AGED MAN	Perhaps they're too busy. Fate has played a joke on you and me.
GIRL	Still a mystery?
MIDDLE-AGED MAN	A woman, no more, no less. A real, living woman.

GIRL	Thank you.
MIDDLE-AGED MAN	I'm the one who should be thankful.
GIRL	*(Coldly.)* Nobody should be thankful to anybody. We should just be glad we're still alive.
MIDDLE-AGED MAN	It's only chance.
GIRL	Why don't you talk about something else?
MIDDLE-AGED MAN	*(Looking at GIRL.)* You're so beautiful and good ... so pretty!
GIRL	Have you only just found out?
MIDDLE-AGED MAN	I only saw you clearly just now. Your body looks splendid in the morning sunlight. It dazzles the eye.
GIRL	Not just the body.
MIDDLE-AGED MAN	You mean your soul's just as beautiful?
GIRL	Don't talk to me about my soul! I wonder if you've got one.
MIDDLE-AGED MAN	Who knows?
GIRL	You only love yourself. *(Silence. She gropes around and finds a T-shirt, which she uses to cover herself. She suddenly covers her face.)* You killed him ...
MIDDLE-AGED MAN	*(Startled.)* I killed him?

GIRL	You. It was you! He was just a kid … *(Sobs.)*
MIDDLE-AGED MAN	*(Resigned.)* He wanted to be a hero. The fool, he killed himself.
GIRL	I hate you! You think you've had me, don't you? But I hate your guts!
MIDDLE-AGED MAN	*(As acrimonious.)* He died because of you. He wanted to prove to my face that I was a coward and that he was a hero. How could I have stopped him? Only you could. Why didn't you stop him? How can you blame me? You're a woman, how come you don't even understand what was happening?
GIRL	Shut up! I won't let you smear him like that …
MIDDLE-AGED MAN	I didn't say you killed him—Don't act like that … *(Tries to console her.)*
GIRL	Don't touch me … I detest you!
MIDDLE-AGED MAN	*(Letting her go.)* I know …
GIRL	You don't know anything. You don't understand anything!
MIDDLE-AGED MAN	*(At a loss what to do.)* Yes … I'm a fool. *(Very troubled.)* Sorry, I'm really sorry.
GIRL	There's nothing to be sorry about … Maybe it really was my fault.
MIDDLE-AGED MAN	Look at you. *(Pitying her.)* You're a good woman, just a bit silly …
GIRL	*(Looking at his miserable face.)* Are we being silly, both of us?

MIDDLE-AGED MAN	*(Puzzled.)* In the face of death we're not heroes, not cowards, not saints, just fools … complete fools.

[GIRL *embraces* MIDDLE-AGED MAN *in silence.*

YOUNG MAN *opens the door a fraction and sneaks in. Then he closes the door again quietly.*

MIDDLE-AGED MAN	Someone's come in!

[*Silence.*

GIRL	*(Turns.)* You're still alive?
YOUNG MAN	*(Leaning against the back of the door.)* They killed the dog, the one sitting on its haunches all night outside the door. It was shot in the middle of the road. *(Silence.)* I chased it away and gave it a kick. The streetlights were already out by then. I couldn't see clearly. I just wanted to try …
MIDDLE-AGED MAN	What took you so long?
YOUNG MAN	I didn't dare come back in straight away. I was afraid I might get noticed. So I ran for a while and turned up an alley. I circled around, trying to find a place to go across, but all the city exits had been blocked by tanks and military vehicles. There were bricks everywhere, and a lot of dead bodies … Give me a cigarette.

[MIDDLE-AGED MAN *puts on his pants, gropes in the pocket, takes out a packet of cigarettes and gives it to* YOUNG MAN. YOUNG MAN *takes one cigarette.* MIDDLE-AGED MAN *takes out a lighter and lights the cigarette for him.* YOUNG MAN *sees that GIRL is naked. Dumbfounded, he does not smoke the cigarette. The lighter goes out.*

YOUNG MAN   *(At a loss.)* Oh ... I ... *(Turns to open the door. About to leave.)*

GIRL   Where are you going?

YOUNG MAN   I ... I don't know ... I just want to go out for a while ...

GIRL   *(Immediately goes over to him barefoot. Pulls at YOUNG MAN's hand and tries to stop him.)* You can't go out! *(To MIDDLE-AGED MAN.)* Block the door, quick!

[MIDDLE-AGED MAN *starts to block the door.*

YOUNG MAN   I just want to take a look ...

GIRL   Silly boy!

YOUNG MAN   I'm not a boy.

GIRL   You are ... You're a silly boy ... *(Holds him in her arms.)*

YOUNG MAN   *(Trying hard to free himself.)* I'm not a boy! I stopped being a boy a long time ago—

GIRL   *(Very tenderly.)* A real macho man, a man who needs a woman's warmth, right?

YOUNG MAN   *(Avoiding GIRL.)* I don't need anybody's pity ... Just give me some peace and quiet!

GIRL   You're overtired. I understand. I'm the same. We're all tired. Living makes people tired ...

[MIDDLE-AGED MAN *lights up cigarette in a corner.*

YOUNG MAN   *(Sobbing. Throws himself into GIRL's arms.)* I ... I shouldn't have come back ...

GIRL	*(Holding him tight.)* Don't say that … You and I are together …. Don't make me worry about you any more … Promise me. Talk to me!
YOUNG MAN	That dog—
GIRL	Never mind the dog.
YOUNG MAN	I shouldn't have—
GIRL	You had nothing to do with it. You're really a silly boy … *(YOUNG MAN kisses her suddenly.)* Oh … Please … I beg you … Don't … Not in front of him—*(She can't free herself, so she lets him kiss her once and then pushes him away.)* That's enough, don't push it—enough! *(Pushes him away with force.)*
YOUNG MAN	*(Still does not let GIRL go.)* How come you let him?
GIRL	Let him what?
YOUNG MAN	You mean you don't know? Who are you trying to fool?
GIRL	I wanted to. I'll do it with anybody I want! As long as I feel like it.
YOUNG MAN	Anybody? Anybody who happens to pass by?
GIRL	It's none of your business.
YOUNG MAN	Even an asshole? Some horny philandering asshole!
GIRL	*(Coldly.)* As long as it's a man.
YOUNG MAN	*(Stunned.)* You sure know how to put on an act! Whore—
	[*GIRL slaps YOUNG MAN in the face. He is about to lose his temper, but seeing that she is squatting down, weeping and biting her hand, he is taken aback and stops.*

MIDDLE-AGED MAN	*(Goes over to* YOUNG MAN *and speaks to him.)* If you don't know how to respect other people, then you don't have any respect for yourself either. *(Throws away his cigarette, goes over to* GIRL, *and supports her with his arm.)*
GIRL	Leave me alone. Just leave me alone. I don't want anybody. Get the hell away from me. You don't deserve a woman's love. You men, you don't deserve any love at all!
	[MIDDLE-AGED MAN *is at a loss, just watching her in silence.*
YOUNG MAN	*(Gingerly walks over to* GIRL.) Look, you're standing in dirty water. I'm sorry …
GIRL	"Sorry, sorry." Always the same old "sorry." Just this one word is enough for a man to hurt a woman.
YOUNG MAN	I was talking nonsense … I take it back, okay? *(Pulls and helps her to her feet.)*
GIRL	No thanks. *(Gets up by herself.)* Nobody can save me. Nobody can save anybody. We're all passers-by. Don't think that just because you pulled me away and saved my life, I should be your woman, and I'll have to sleep with you.
YOUNG MAN	I didn't say that.
GIRL	You're right. You didn't say it, that is, you didn't say it out loud. But I know what you're thinking. You think that women are cheap, right? That they can't live without men? You're just a little boy, but you've got such a filthy mind.

YOUNG MAN	*(Uneasy.)* I just wanted … wanted to see you again. I shouldn't have come back … I was afraid I'd never see you again … never find you … never know where you were … I was alone. If I could cross the roads successfully, it'd be all right, and if I couldn't … and if I were shot to death, it'd be all right too. It would've been so quick. I just wanted to see you again … to have another look at you.… I haven't really had a good look at you …
GIRL	*(Stroking* YOUNG MAN's *head.)* Me too, I was worried about you …
YOUNG MAN	We'll never part from each other. Even if we die, we'll die together!
GIRL	I'd only be a burden to you. You should run while you still can. Never mind me.
YOUNG MAN	Then I'll stay, I won't go anywhere. *(Buries his head in* GIRL's *chest.)*
	[MIDDLE-AGED MAN *gathers his clothes.*]
GIRL	What are you doing?
MIDDLE-AGED MAN	I'm going.
GIRL	You're not a child. Why do you act like one?
MIDDLE-AGED MAN	I just don't want to be in the way.
GIRL	Are you saying that we're in your way?
MIDDLE-AGED MAN	We're in each other's way. It's better for us to part.

GIRL	Because of him?
MIDDLE-AGED MAN	No, because of me.
GIRL	*(Scoffing.)* You're in your own way?
MIDDLE-AGED MAN	Perhaps. Anyway, you two were here first.
YOUNG MAN	Nobody's asking you to go.
MIDDLE-AGED MAN	Of course not.
YOUNG MAN	You can stay and just mind your own business.
MIDDLE-AGED MAN	Thank you for letting me stay—
GIRL	*(Coldly.)* Everybody's on the run. No one's the boss here.
MIDDLE-AGED MAN	*(Smiles bitterly.)* True. But this is no heaven.
GIRL	And no hell either.
MIDDLE-AGED MAN	Of course not. And we've got a beautiful young woman here.
GIRL	A real live woman.
MIDDLE-AGED MAN	A kind woman.
GIRL	Who knows? Maybe she's a wanton woman.
MIDDLE-AGED MAN	There doesn't seem to be any absolute defining line, generally speaking.

GIRL	Men are the same. To women, there's no absolute defining line between a hero and a jerk.
MIDDLE-AGED MAN	Especially in front of a naked woman.
GIRL	You really talk dirty. *(Silence.)* How come you've got nothing to say any more? You're so smart, eh? I'm talking about men in general, maybe about all men. *(To YOUNG MAN.)* And that includes you. You're only slightly better than he is, because you've preserved a bit of innocence. But you men are all the same inside. You think that women are all bad, but it's you who are the dirty ones. You only feel good after you've made women dirty, but in actual fact you've only managed to make yourselves dirty.
MIDDLE-AGED MAN	Everyone's got desires. There's no difference between men and women in that respect.
GIRL	But do men have women's kindness? You've got a one-track mind, you only want to possess and to take. Have you thought of giving women anything? And women, besides their duties as women, are also mothers. They're always so tolerant, even though your greed is insatiable, and they're hurt again and again.
MIDDLE-AGED MAN	Don't forget women are also daughters.
GIRL	All the more reason not to hurt them!
YOUNG MAN	Can we talk about something else?

MIDDLE-AGED MAN	You don't have to listen. Listening to women talking philosophy is infinitely more interesting than listening to men arguing about politics.
GIRL	Men don't have a monopoly on philosophy.
MIDDLE-AGED MAN	I'm not saying that women can't talk philosophy. Philosophy's an intellectual game, something to do when we're coasting along in life and we've got nothing better to do. Both men and women can talk philosophy *ad infinitum*. But women have women's philosophy, and men have theirs; neither can solve any problems.
GIRL	*(To YOUNG MAN.)* Don't move. Just lie there. You're looking like a good kid.
MIDDLE-AGED MAN	*(Bitterly. To YOUNG MAN.)* It's real fun to listen to a woman talking philosophy like this.
GIRL	As if you haven't had your fun before. *(MIDDLE-AGED MAN just waves his hand, without saying anything.)* You'll never have anything! You're always high above everybody else, looking at people with your cold eyes. You've no kindness, no love. You're destined to be alone. I'm sure that even when you're making love with a woman, you can't win her heart!
	[*MIDDLE-AGED MAN is furious. He is at a loss for words. He just keeps moving around.*]
GIRL	*(Challenging MIDDLE-AGED MAN.)* I see, there are actually times when you've got nothing to say. Don't walk back and forth like that. You're making too much noise with the water.
MIDDLE-AGED MAN	*(Angrily.)* You're the devil!

GIRL	You made me!
MIDDLE-AGED MAN	*(Shocked.)* Me?
GIRL	Yes, you. You'll never understand a woman!
MIDDLE-AGED MAN	Maybe … *(Heaves a sigh.)* You're right. *(Stares at the water which covers the entire floor. Simply steps into the water and sits down. Lowers his head.)*

[YOUNG MAN, *nestled in* GIRL's *chest, starts to sob.*

GIRL	Don't hold your feelings back. Just cry your heart out. They can't hear you outside. It's already daylight. They won't come for us now.
YOUNG MAN	I … I love you …
GIRL	Don't talk about love … *(Sadly.)* Love is already dead.…
YOUNG MAN	I want to come out of here with you alive. We've got to carry on living. I want to be with you forever. We'll get away from this ghastly place, we'll go and hide in the country, in the mountains! I'll treasure and care for you, I won't hurt you any more …
GIRL	But I'm not worthy of your love … you understand? I just feel for you, a bit …
YOUNG MAN	I love you!
GIRL	*(Shocked.)* No, don't say that!
YOUNG MAN	What do you want me to say then? I want you—
GIRL	Oh! *(Moved. Bends down to kiss him.)*

[*Girl and Young Man hug each other and kiss passionately. Middle-aged Man walks toward the door quietly. He bumps into some object, which falls down with a bang. Startled, Girl and Young Man immediately move apart.*

Middle-aged Man	*(Apologetic.)* I'm sorry. I didn't do it on purpose.
Young Man	*(Cannot control his anger.)* If you want to go, just go quickly. Get the hell out of here!
Middle-aged Man	You'll have plenty of time after I open the door and get out, son. *(Girl laughs coldly.)* What are you laughing at? *(Getting angry.)* It's not funny!
Girl	I'm laughing at you! You think that is all I want? *(Laughs hysterically.)*
Middle-aged Man	*(Uneasy.)* No. *(Embarrassed.)* I'm just trying to hide … from myself.
Girl	Then just open the door. Open the door and get the hell out! But you're afraid of dying —
Middle-aged Man	*(Fighting back.)* Death isn't that horrifying if we're destined to die. What's horrifying is despair, the despair before dying, when we can't tolerate one another. It's this sort of hysteria that's the most horrifying—
Girl	It's you, your self that's the most horrifying! Wherever your escape to, you can't escape from your self! *(Sympathetically.)* You're afraid of being left alone. Who isn't afraid of being alone? Come over here. You're just a big boy who needs someone to comfort him. *(Young Man gets up in anger.)* What's come over you blowing your top like that?

YOUNG MAN	So depressing!
GIRL	*(Cannot control herself.)* You're all depressed. When you've dumped your troubles onto women, every one of you is a hero. You can't stand loneliness, but you demand that women be alone. You can't face yourselves, and the only thing you can do is prove that you're a man, a real man in front of women, but you won't allow a woman to prove herself, that she's a woman, a woman with integrity, dignity, and desires! *(Stands up. Proudly.)* You only allow yourselves to have desires, but you won't allow a woman, someone you possess, someone you claim to love, to have desires for anything but you. You only allow yourselves to have your so-called freedom, spirit, and will, but you won't allow other people to have them. You just pass on your pain to others—Every one of you is selfish, ugly, and wretched, and dying to show off your ego. *(Laughs to herself.)* You're only real when you're in front of women, the naked bodies of women, and when you're naked as well.
MIDDLE-AGED MAN	*(Softly.)* You're playing with fire.
GIRL	*(Softly.)* Playing with death, for once. *(Turns and talks to herself.)* Before death arrives, a woman is already destroyed by the man she loves … *(Closes her eyes.)*

[MIDDLE-AGED MAN *thinks for a while, then throws down his clothes, walks over to* GIRL *and stands in front of her. He embraces her and starts to kiss her. She nestles into his arms.*

Young Man is agitated. He cannot restrain himself from rushing over to them. He embraces Girl in a frenzy, wrestling her onto the ground, and the two of them roll around in the muddy water. First she moans, then howls loudly like a wounded animal. Middle-aged Man moves away to one side and stares at the two twisting bodies, looking very sad. Everything happens slowly and solemnly, accompanied by the continuous sound of dripping water.

GIRL   *(Her voice muffled.)* No! No—You're crazy! I don't—I can't—Don't —*(Faints.)*

YOUNG MAN   *(Frightened.)* What's wrong with you? *(Kneels down beside her and shakes her forcefully.)* Wake up! Wake up! *(Scared.)* She—?

[*Middle-aged Man walks over, squats down, and gently caresses Girl's limp arms. The sound of water continues, as the water level is getting higher. Girl slowly turns, wakes up from her unconsciousness and wails tearfully.*

GIRL   *(Slowly getting to her feet, she ignores the two men and sits in the muddy water in bewilderment.)* Such desolation …

[*Middle-aged Man takes out his cigarettes and puts one into his mouth. He is about to light up.*

GIRL   *(Without looking at Middle-aged Man.)* Any more?

[*Middle-aged Man hands the packet of cigarettes to Girl, who takes it and pulls one cigarette out. He lights it for her. The cigarette in her hand falls into the water. She takes out another one and throws it into the water. One after another she throws away all the cigarettes. Finally, she also throws the empty cigarette packet into the water. She sits down motionless, her face upturned, puzzled and cold. MIDDLE-AGED MAN stares at the lighter in his hand. He turns up the flame to its highest. YOUNG MAN kneels in the water, his head lowered and his back toward the two of them.*

The morning sun shines through the cracks in the roof, dyeing the dirty water red.

MIDDLE-AGED MAN throws the lighter into the water, forgetting that he still has a cigarette in his mouth.

Heavy pounding on the door, which sounds like the rapid firing of a machine gun:

Bang, bang, bang!

Bang, bang,

Bang, bang, bang, bang, bang!

The three are motionless, sitting quietly in the dirty water which looks like blood.]

Paris, October 1989

Notes and Suggestions for Performing *Escape*

1. Since ancient times, human existence has been an unending tragedy. Our play is an attempt to express modern man's dilemma in the classical tragedy form. The performance should be infused with the solemnity of ritual and adopt the recitative style common in the tragedy of fate in Greek theatre.

2. *Escape* is about the psychology of political philosophy. It should not be made into a play of socialist realism, which seeks only to mirror contemporary political incidents. The actors should avoid representing the reality of the trivialities in everyday living. Their movements should be clean and simple.

3. As for the set, lighting, and costumes, the predominant colors should be black, white and gray, richly layered. Bright colors only appear at the end of the play.

4. Music is not necessary. Sounds of real objects can be used and given musical rendition.

5. A word about the puddle and the pool, which is the result of the puddle extending. The stage can be covered with a layer of waterproof material. The volume of water does not have to be big; it can be similar to that which comes from a common household tap to maintain a water level of around three to five centimeters in various places. There is no need for a huge pool with a large amount of water.

About *Escape*

In June 1989 after the Tiananmen Incident, a friend asked me if I could write a play for an American theater company. The play should be about China and, of course, related to reality. I agreed. In August the first batch of exiles from Beijing arrived in Paris and among them were a few of my old friends. At the end of September, I started to write the play and finished it a month later. The theater company read the English translation and requested revision. I refused and had my friend pass on my words: Even the Communist Party could not coerce me into making changes to my manuscripts when I was in China, let alone an American theater company. Now the Royal Dramatic Theatre of Sweden is enthusiastic about staging *Escape*, for this I would like to express my heartfelt gratitude.

Escape was published in the first issue of the Chinese literary journal *Jintian* 今天 [Today] when it resumed publication overseas. Recent news coming out of China reported that the Communist government had classified the journal as a reactionary publication, and that it had taken away my party membership and state appointment. I would only say that their decision came too late: Two years ago when they opened fire on the people, I already announced in Paris my withdrawal from the Chinese Communist Party.

The play also came under attack by some of my acquaintances in the Democracy Movement. This was expected to happen since in the play I had criticized some of its immature tendencies. A few my writer friends also disapproved of the play from another angle, claiming that it was too political to be pure literature. Without doubt I am no political activist, nor do I think that literature should serve politics, but that does not preclude me from referring to politics in my writings when I want to. It is only advocacy literature to which I object—the kind of literature that is strapped to the war chariot of a particular political camp. A writer has his own tasks to do.

My intention of writing this play was not confined to censuring the massacre. I stated in the postscript that *Escape* is not a socialist realist play. I believe that being alive means always on the run, either away from political persecution or from other people. One still has to run away from one's self, which, once awakened, is precisely what one can never run away from—This is the tragedy of modern man.

In his book *Éloge de la fuite*, the contemporary French thinker Henri Laborit opines that when the different forces of resistance converge into a collective, the individual will immediately be reduced to servility inside that collective. Escape, Laborit concludes, is thus the only way out. I share his point of view. For a writer, and for any individual, unwavering independence is of the utmost importance, without which there is no freedom to speak of. Escape is nothing unusual to the writer— I accept this fact with ease, and for the rest of my life I do not aspire to return to a so-called motherland under authoritarian rule.

One's misfortune comes not only from political repression, social customs, fads, and the will of others. As I see it, it is also derived from the self. The self is not God. It should neither be suppressed nor worshipped. That is what it is, and we can never run away from it. Such is the destiny of mankind. The classical Greek tragedies of fate and Shakespearian tragedies about the individual indeed share the same source with the tragedies that deal with the self of modern man. This explains why I have adoped a pure tragic form for *Escape*.

Neither a naturalistic nor realistic approach to this play is recommended. As in *Dubai* 獨白 [Soliloquy], another play of mine read today by Mr. Björn Granath, the director of *Escape*, I suggest that the actor should maintain a certain distance from the character he is playing, so that he is able to observe his own performance from the side, and move in and out of his character from time to time. Both theatricality and appropriate ritualisticity are essential during a performance. Over the past few days I have been working with the director, producer, set designer, and actors on the rehearsal plan for *Escape*. I was greatly relieved and delighted by their understanding of my ideas.

At a gathering of some Chinese writers in Oslo last year, I said that films and televisions proliferate in the present age. Literature—of course I refer to nonconsumerist literature—is increasingly a personal matter. This is especially true for those Chinese exile writers who write in Chinese. Writing has become a luxury, and one must have a willingness to be lonely.

Thank you for coming today. I did not expect there would be such a large audience. I would also like to extend my thanks to Professor Göran Malmqvist, who has translated my works into Swedish.

Gao Xingjian's speech at the Royal Dramatic Theatre of Sweden, Stockholm, May 26, 1991.
Published in the Supplement of *United Daily News*, June 17, 1991.

Translated into English by Shelby K. Y. Chan

Performance History of *Escape* (written 1989)

PERFORMANCE

1992   Kungliga Dramatiska Teatern. Stockholm, Sweden. Directed by Björn Granath.

1992   Nürnberg Theater. Nürnberg, Germany. Directed by Johannes Klett.

1992   Magasin d'Ecriture Théâtrale. Communauté française de Belgique. Directed by Jean-Claude Idée.

1994   RA Theatre Company. Tours, France. Directed by Madelaine Gautiche.

1994   Teatr polski. Poznan, Poland. Directed by Edward Wojtaszek.

1997   Ryunokai Gekidan. Osaka, Kobe, Tokyo, Japan.

1998   Atelier Nomande. Benin, Ivory Coast.

1998   Haiyuza Gekidan. Tokyo, Japan.

2002   Théâtre National Quatrième Art. Tunis, Tunisia.

2002   Arts Club Theatre Company, Granville Island. Vancouver, Canada.

RADIO BROADCAST

1992   British Broadcasting Corporation. London, UK.

1997   Radio France Culture. Paris, France.

PLAY READING

1992   Institute of Contemporary Arts. London, UK. Read by Gao Xingjian.

1992   Festival International des Francophonies. Limoges, France.

Compiled by Shelby K. Y. Chan

The Man
Who Questions
Death

叩問死亡

Characters

THIS MAN Old and neurotic.

THAT MAN Older and weaker than THIS MAN, cold and unemotional.

THIS MAN and THAT MAN, both wearing black shirts and pants, are one and the same character. Their acting is clean and simple, and their movements are smooth and unhindered. Sometimes the words they speak cut across one another as if engaged in a dialogue, but these are actually the monologue of the same character. They can observe each other but their eyes should never meet.

Stage

Only a few ready-made objects will suffice, for instance, a supermarket pushcart (gilded if needed), a female doll (the best is the inflatable kind made of rubber), and a garbage can found on the street.

THIS MAN   Hello!

Anybody home?

Hello—

No answer, not a soul.

Not even security?

Can someone open the door? Please open the door!

Well, I guess I'm stuck in here ... a public place for all to see. A modern art museum—or shall we say a contemporary art museum. But it's all locked up, and locked up tight.

Seriously, you're not going to lock up your visitors, are you? It's just too much.

I missed the train, and there was more than one hour to kill before the next one arrived. I thought I'd go for a stroll on the street. I went out of the station, walked along the main street, and saw the front door of this place wide open, so I came in to take a look. I meant to buy a ticket, but there wasn't anybody at the counter.... That was how you got locked up for no reason. Ridiculous, wasn't it?

Such bad luck! Guards! Watchmen! A visitor is being locked up in the museum, with your precious works of art. Hey, aren't you concerned at all?

[*Lifts his head and looks around.*

You've got security cameras covering every corner, right? How come you haven't noticed an intruder? You know, he might even damage your objets d'art. Is your security system broken? Or are your cameras just decorations, to scare the thieves away?

No matter what, you've got to let people leave this treasure palace of yours!

I really don't have time to fool around. I've got a train to catch. Really got to go now. Go check your opening hours on the front door. There's still ten more minutes before closing. This is a public institution, you know. You can't lock your doors just like that. It's not yet time … We the taxpayers are paying your bills.

You've got to have some sense of civic responsibility. Your taste in art? I really don't give a damn. You can collect what you want and all you want, but you've no right to collect people and lock them up!

I don't care how you label yourself: art nouveau, anti-art, non-art or whatever—even conceptual art or invisible art; but Mr. Curator, you can't turn people into your collection without their prior consent. No, you can't do that. Even if I didn't object to this game you're playing, being a nice guy and all, you shouldn't make me miss my train. As if you haven't caused me enough trouble already!

Mr. Curator, let me tell you something: If your surveillance system's still working, then you should take a really good look at this. I'm going to smash your windows and wreck your doors, then I'm going to bust out of this prison of yours. Cultural prison, artistic prison, I don't care what it's supposed to be. For me, it's turned into spiritual bondage, it's impeding my personal freedom! If you insist on locking me up like a prisoner ... hah! I'm going to go wild and do all sorts of crazy things!

[*Silence.*

I guess everybody's gone. Really, they should've made sure that no one's left on the premises before closing up. Looks like this place only gets a few visitors in the first place, except when there's an opening or something. What a nice cushy job you've got!

[*Silence. THIS MAN listens intently.*

Maybe it's raining. Nothing here ... boring as hell. Who'd come in, except to shelter from the rain?

[*Shouts.*

Stupid, really stupid! I'm pissed off!

[*Silence.*

Silence ... with sound-proofing like this, no wonder there's no reaction whatsoever. Scarier than a ghost town!

[*Silence, longer than before.*

Okay, what do you want to do? Wait until tomorrow, until they find out that someone's locked inside and ask the police to interrogate you? Or do you want to call the police yourself? But you need to have a cell phone first. The gadget is so annoying, but you've got to have one, especially when you've been taken hostage.

[*Silence.*

You should find an alarm. Maybe get hold of a bottle of gas and set the place on fire. That'd trigger the smoke detector the ceiling all right. But then how would you explain that you didn't intend to steal anything, nor did you want to set the place on fire. And they'd also accuse you of barging in without a ticket too! Then who'd vouch for you, that you've got no criminal intent?

Or you could sit tight like a good kid and spend the night among this junk, also known as art to some people. You'd get so pissed off that you'd rather die!

[*Hits one exhibit.*

Maybe you could kill some time doing this, and enjoy yourself to boot. There's no point shouting at the top of your lungs, because nobody'll hear you. Might as well take a look around, and see for yourself why the so-called contemporary art has fallen so low!

[*Hits the exhibit again.*

You've got to investigate. Or shall we say you have to diagnose this contagious disease, that is, before you yourself get infected. You'll have to stay up all night, but come tomorrow morning will you still be fresh and alert?

[*Takes a short rest.*

Even if this museum closes down because of mismanagement or shortage of funds, and they don't have money to waste anymore, or if it is closed temporarily for renovation, you're already in their clutches. Just like a fly caught inside a glass window case, you'll die for lack of air. You'll become a sample, a piece of dehydrated art, and your skeleton will be put in good use, to fill the gap in their exhibition.

[*Laughs loudly and hits a certain exhibit continuously.*

You can't help congratulating yourself. You've been picked, chosen! How lucky!

They'd hidden themselves in the ticket counter to watch you. They let you in without a ticket, then, just like that, they were able to lock you up. And you have no way of explaining yourself. Look at this guy, a free exhibit, free of charge! There are urinals made in France and the United States, also Asian imports, odds and ends, from brand new refrigerators to a hodgepodge of stuff one finds in junk shops, cigarette butts, and even used sanitary napkins. Anything goes, no matter how broken or damaged, as long as they don't stink. If worst comes to worst, they could be sterilized and used again, which is called "recycling." There are all kinds of exhibits but no living human beings. Why not?

[*Hits the exhibit hard several times.*

All that crap's made its way into the museum and found itself listed in beautifully appointed catalogs and analyzed with the latest critical jargon. Why should poor human beings, the dirtiest and most evil creatures in the universe, be left out in the cold? No question about it, you should have a place in this museum!

[*Claps his hands.*

Yes, you, you're the one! You've been nabbed.

[*Laughs out loud.*

A live exhibit, a human, what a wonderful idea! From every angle, anthropological or anthropomorphical, this event's so big that it should be made into a DVD and covered widely by all the media.

[*Very excited. Claps his hands continuously.*

Suddenly you've become world news, you're as famous as a football star. You don't even have to go through years of hard training, play countless matches, or worry about getting your bones broken. Just like a kite, you soar up straight into the clouds, and then you land safely, having secured a place in art almanacs. As long as the organizers have enough money for advertising, they'll keep touting you as the first human exhibit, and your name will be recorded in future volumes of art history.

[*Takes a rest, gasping for breath.*

Of course like everybody else you can't help being narcissistic, an exquisite objet d'art that's been chosen, accepted and admired, an archetype which the imagination, no matter how fanciful, cannot create, a work praised and appraised, analyzed, deconstructed layer by layer, and heaped on with hitherto unprecedented kudos, higher than all that's been accorded to any existing work. No doubt about it, you're absolutely convincing, enough to make the critics and art historians babble on and on with their endless critiques, exegeses, and contentious arguments …

[*A bit tired, takes a breather.*

But you can't help falling behind. It's already too late. Of course, you know that nowadays you have to be in the limelight, to get people to notice you. It doesn't matter what you do. You can masturbate in front of the camera or you can throw yourself out of the window onto the street. Of course you're not really killing yourself in the process. You only want to put yourself in the record books. As your audience awaits you down on the street, you land safety and comfortably onto the stack of carefully arranged foam cushions already prepared. With that, your name is entered into art history. As for latecomers keen on making the big time, they'll have to get rid of everyone and everything!

[*He picks up a bowling ball from the shopping cart and throws it away. It hits something with a loud boom.*

To hell with ancestors! Wipe out everything that's old! Take out all rivals! In this way the artistic revolution is accomplished.

Eradicate all who came before you. This method is absolutely foolproof; it delivers every time, and it doesn't matter if it's political or artistic revolution. History has been made this way: Like bowling, you get points with every strike.

[*Picks up another ball and throws it away, making a louder boom.*

Look, if you want to make people take note of you, you've got to come out shining! If you want to be famous, trample on others, walk over them, crush them, burn them, cut them up, pluck them and root them out completely!

History has been written with blood and violence. Mind you, art history is much tamer. You fire your shots at the masters, and you'll make a name for yourself. Just like the father who teaches his son how to shoot at the fun fair, someday the son will turn around, shoot the father and take over as head of the family. Overthrow God, take his place and be the Creator. It's all the same.

[*Knocks down the shopping cart, making a loud bang.*

God is dead, and people scramble to replace him. It's only natural. Everybody wants to be God, or claims that he is Jesus Christ. God has only one son. But lo and behold! So many saviors have popped up on this wretched Earth of ours. The son of God was born with a mission to save the world, because our world, having been created, is not perfect, which causes everyone to suffer. So we have a great need for saviors … Human beings are born to suffer, even if we refuse to admit that we have the responsibility to save our country and its people, we still have to save our own souls. Such is man's destiny.

The question is: Do you really have a soul? And who can save this soul of yours? O Lord, have mercy on us!

[*Laughs loudly and continuously.*

The way you talk! But you know, that's exactly what you've been wanting to say!

[*Laughs so hard that he is gasping.*

You and your behavioral art, you're just trying to roll out the little bit of cleverness in you. But who can give you any feedback?

[*Stops laughing.*

You refuse to go on display like an exhibit, but you still want to show off your talent, more or less, to confirm your identity. The question is: Do you have any?

[*Motionless.*

You think that it's a matter of course, because you consider yourself infallible. At the same time you've also come to a self-understanding—You know that you just can't become God. So you resort to metaphysics and dabble in philosophy, claiming that "You think, therefore you are." Sure, you have to be eloquent to justify yourself; remember that words are the raw materials of thinking, but your problem is that you have nothing worth saying. So you try to bluff your way through with word games, as if you were playing mahjong. One way or another you find yourself a beginning, and like stringing beads along a piece of thread, you string words into sentences, then group them into concepts, and combine the concepts to make up a theory, which becomes part of an ideology, but it's just a never-never land, like the moon's reflection in the water. However, it's not so easy to become a thinker, so you put on an act, pretending that you're thoughtful and deep. This isn't so much cheating as satisfying your own ego, a rather harmless form of self-gratification.

In fact, you clearly know that your mind is a total void. You can't say what's missing in there, love or lust, but nonetheless you're tormented beyond words. Or else, you wouldn't have blown up like that, like a rat scurrying around because it can't find a hole to sneak into, or a cat locked in a cage, desperately screeching, trying to claw its way out. Even animals would react when they're in a fix like that, and poor humans, who are willful, neurotic, greedy and vain, of course they'd scream and make a scene. If that still leads them nowhere, they'd have to do themselves in.

[*Becoming angry and hysterical.*

So you declare: the day of judgment has arrived. And since God is already dead, the artists who have destroyed art have to face their own death as well.

Mr. Curator, that's exactly what you want to put on display, isn't it? It's so funny—If you really want to promote your museum, the best way is to close it down. Art is already dead, Mr. Curator, so the construction of your institute was an exercise in futility, built for no other purpose than to put an end to art. You should know that even before you started your job, art had been tortured and put to death. When artists proclaimed the death of God and bestowed upon themselves the title of Creator, art was at the brink of extinction. Your museum is nothing but a graveyard. You may as well turn it into a supermarket—Come to think of it, you've done that already. The idea is not new any more, it's passé. The thing is, your supermarket–museum can't be any more vulgar than it is now, it'd be too easy. Even the public, whom you claim to serve, feels bored by your antics, so you can only serve yourself. You ignore the visitors that you ought to inspire, yet you challenge those artists genuinely dedicated to art, telling them to give up their places to these worthless dregs.

Art isn't really dead; only the art in your museum has died. Let's go back to what we said, Mr. Curator. It's not that you were capable of causing art to wane and die. You don't have the talent. You only managed to compile a name list for the artistic revolution, and etch out the names of the revolutionaries onto their gravestones. Oh, all glories be to the butchers of art!

[*As* THIS MAN *spreads his arms in proclamation, his back facing the audience,* THAT MAN *appears on the opposite side.*

THAT MAN   Are you through with your endless proclamation? Don't you feel the least bit tired? Your protest, your eloquence, and your moral anger, what good will they do?

You're just a passerby. In the middle of this moonlit night you find yourself locked behind the iron bars like a prisoner. If you hadn't missed your train, you wouldn't have been in this kind of mess. There's no need for such ranting. It's all in your destiny. At any rate, you've brought it on yourself. If it happens, it happens, even though sometimes it happens by chance. You can't escape even if you want to. In short, it's a combination of many factors. Maybe nothing's purely accidental, except when cars collide, planes crash, bombs explode above our heads, or guns misfire, all of which nobody can predict. What's absolutely certain is that you'll have to die sooner or later. Death is waiting for you, whatever you do or don't do. There's no escape from this ending.

[*THAT MAN smiles rather coldly.*

No matter your pose, no matter your fancy steps, which you consider so interesting, they will ultimately fall into the Big Void, ending up in nothingness. Isn't this always the case? Death: it's the worst of the worst, the lowest of the low.

[*THAT MAN giggles happily.*

The only thing you can grasp is this tiny bit of understanding: Sooner or later you'll have to die. What incentive is there to live on?

You can't even grasp your own self. If this were a piece of straw, it can't save your life when you're drowning, no matter how desperately you cling to it. You can only maintain your life now with self-observation, keeping an eye on death, this most meaningless death, which gobbles up everything like a bottomless black hole.

[*THAT MAN moves closer and closer to THIS MAN.*

You're getting older by the day; you can't turn back the clock. The latest techniques and medications that claim to make you young again can do nothing except make you go bankrupt. Sooner or later you'll turn into a corpse. There's not much you can do; if you're still mentally capable and financially viable, you can find yourself an insurance company, sign a contract, and choose a plot and a gravestone from their catalog. Then you dutifully pay your installments by the month, by the quarter, or by the year. Ah, when a man grows old, it's more terrifying than death!

Who could rid you of your worries for you? Nobody, only you yourself can do it. Be happy and make merry before death arrives; if nothing else, it's one way to entertain yourself. How self-defeating can you get!

[*This Man, up to now with his back facing the audience, starts to do a little jig. Then he moves away and watches That Man intently.*

Man is destined to die; you can't do anything about it. You make yourself busy, running around doing this and that, only to keep yourself entertained ....

[*This Man stops dancing.*

You're too old; you can't even move your legs. The only thing you're able to do is to keep rambling on endlessly, only then can you feel that you're still alive.

You want to make a lot of noise, just to prove that you really exist, but who'd verify it? What's the use?

You shout at the top of your voice, just to punish yourself, and then you plan to give up everything once and for all!

No, that's not right. Better to say that you're just trying to look for a little happiness in your boredom.

[*This Man still has his back facing the audience. He takes hold of a rubber doll and dances with it.*

This is exactly what you've been hoping for, but you can't find a woman to hold in your arms. You make love but you don't feel the pleasure. You only have a glimmer of life in you, and you can't even live it with relish, so you find yourself a substitute. You're drifting as if you were in a dream, but you don't know where you're drifting to.

[*THIS MAN puts the deflated rubber doll on the floor. THAT MAN stands still and takes a glance at the doll.*

A shriveled corpse!

[*THIS MAN takes away the doll's hairpiece, revealing its bald head.*

You only wanted a whore, nothing more, a woman who's as corrupted and depraved as you are, a faceless body which has lost its soul, to satisfy that little bit of desire in you, so that you could disappear inside the pitch-black abyss....

[*THAT MAN moves forward, picks up the doll, and shows it to the audience before dumping it.*

Hasn't even got a hole in it!

[*THAT MAN gives THIS MAN a cold smile.*

It arouses your desire, and then it leaves you high and dry and makes you sick to the stomach!

You can't stop it, you're getting older and weaker by the day, you're frittering your life away. The women you once had already left you a long time ago. There are no more hands to hold you, to caress you, or to give you a little tenderness. At this moment, it makes no difference whether you're dead or alive. Nobody will ever think of you. The past is no more, all dissolved in your memories. What was missed can't be had again, there's no remedy. Remorse and regrets are futile. Your whole life is wasted and meaningless, and you can't live it one more time.

But do you really want to start your life again at your age? It's too late. The time has passed for you to start all over. You fall and you pick yourself up again. Easier said than done. Gather up your strength and fight. But for what?

First, you don't have any woman; second, you don't have any children, and you've lost contact with the few acquaintances you had. You can't understand why you're so alone in the world. Even ghosts ignore you. If you were to have a sudden heart attack, you'd be through once and for all at this very moment. The only link you have with this world is a piece of paper, your I.D. card. If it were burned, they'd have no way of knowing who you are. They'd wrap you up and take you away: The place would then be cleaned up and you'd vanish without a trace.

[*This Man takes out a card and lights it up with his lighter. That Man looks up.*

A piece of paper blowing in the wind. Your life's just like that. The paper has to fall down sooner or later. Who can stop it from falling?

[*THIS MAN lets go of what is left of the burning card, which falls onto the stage. When THAT MAN lowers his head, THIS MAN picks up a piece of rope from the floor.*

A piece of rope. You pick it up. You pull at it and you drag it along. What are you going to do with it?

[*THIS MAN runs around the stage, dragging the rope behind him.*

You're straining yourself, your back's aching all over. You're totally exhausted, half dead, with nothing to show for your troubles.

[*THIS MAN throws away the rope.*

You've stopped. Why not? You have every reason to do so.

You've been busy climbing up the ladder all your life, going up and down again and again. Now in your twilight years, what do you see besides the darkness in the world?

[*THIS MAN walks backward, stumbling left and right.*

Throughout your life, it was either people trampling on you or you squashing other people. Good or bad, you tried to find a way out among the bustling crowd, not knowing year after year if this long journey would ever come to an end.

When you look back at all that's behind you, it's all one big haziness, except for a few fading memories of things past.

[*THIS MAN feels bored. He takes out a small piece of paper from his pocket and blows on it, making it fly in the air.*

A small piece of paper is drifting in the air without rhyme or reason. It's interesting to look at it before it touches the ground. Why? Not because there's anything special about the paper itself, but because someone is looking.

[*When THIS MAN is watching the falling paper, a projection of a plastic bag floating in the air appears on top of the stage.*

Even if it were only a plastic bag, or just a garbage bag dancing in the wind, it's still interesting to watch!

The look in your eyes imparts meaning; otherwise, all the things in the world would be so boring, so mundane.

[*The projection on top of the stage disappears. THAT MAN opens his eyes wide and moves back. The stage turns dark, accentuating THIS MAN's silhouette.*

THIS MAN   That guy is waiting for you to go over there. You go forward, he goes back. You take one step forward, he takes one step back, no more, no less, just to lure you into his trap one step at a time.

He lures you into his illusion, made of a sliver of light and nothing else. But it makes you happy and you follow him, moving around joyfully in circles.

This old man, you know him only too well, but you let him push you around and manipulate you. You can't help it. Why? Because you can't stand being lonely.

He's made you look like his lover. He's evil to the core. He's as filthy as the world we're in, with only one appreciable difference: The world is unknowing, and he is very much self-aware.

[*THAT MAN is pleased with himself, his body swaying slightly.*

You follow him, and you begin to dance, your steps staggering in a zigzag.

And you start humming a song, a martial tune: "Be a real man, to the battlefield here I come." You make up the song as you go along. There's really nothing worth singing about, but you still sing out loud. You simply want to get some relief, to let out the surging feeling of regret in your heart.

You feel compelled to utter some sound. It's a kind of need, just as people need to breathe, some need to write, and all need to take a piss.

[*THAT MAN stops swaying, becoming motionless. The following dialogues are spoken one after another as in a conversation, but the eyes of the two characters do not meet.*

THAT MAN   It's getting too late!

THIS MAN   What's too late?

THAT MAN   What's past is past. There's no use having regrets.

THIS MAN   Man only lives once. We're all like that.

THAT MAN   That's true.

THIS MAN   Once you miss the chance, that's it. You can't do anything to take it back. Everybody knows.

THAT MAN	That's why you have to think carefully. It'll be too late if you leave it till the very end, after you've wasted everything away. Think about it while there's time, when things are about to be destroyed but still not yet destroyed.
THIS MAN	That's why you hesitate, and you can't make up your mind. You're holding your breath to gather strength, but you don't know which foot you should step out first.
THAT MAN	That's right. Sometimes you really have to halt your steps and stop rushing to this place or that, especially at your age. When you're going downhill in your life, you have to learn how to apply the brake in a hurry. Before you make up your mind, whether the decision is a yes, a no, or a maybe, you have to think thrice. Even if you die, you have to die for the right reason, the right cause, and without regret, even though you have no doubt that the ending's already been decided, and that it won't make any difference one way or the other. When you've lifted your foot but still haven't put it down, the moment of indecision brings up all kinds of interesting feelings, feelings that are worth savoring. Right?
THIS MAN	At that moment you feel whatever is going to be wasted is the most precious, and whatever you're going to miss out on is the most cherished, even though in the end you'll still waste it and miss out on it. You can't go back no matter what.
THAT MAN	Exactly! Once something's gone, you can't bring it back. When it's gone it's finished. Past happiness and love

are like shadows in the water, they can't give you any warmth, and they'll break as soon as you try to fish them out with your fingers. Lingering in the past is like taking drugs.

THIS MAN   That's why you don't want to be tormented like this. Living your days in memories only deceives yourself and others. No, you don't want to search your memories, to commit a slow suicide in this way.

THAT MAN   But then again what is there that's worth remembering? What you lived through, no matter how beautiful, can't be relived, and what you missed will only lead to endless regrets. Either way, it's futile and meaningless; they only inflict excruciating pain on you.

THIS MAN   Of course you'll never do such stupid things. You don't regret and you don't repent. You've pushed aside heartaches and feelings of despair. You live for today, just doing what you have to do and what you can do!

THAT MAN   But what can you do at your age? You've already one foot in the grave, what is it that you have to do and are able to do? That's the question.

THIS MAN   True. It's too late.

THAT MAN   *C'est la vie!*

THIS MAN   But you can always have a new start....

THAT MAN   A new start for what? To live your life again, and again let it go to waste? Let me give you some advice: Forget all about the past, just wait and see what the future will bring.

THIS MAN	Wouldn't that be muddling through life?
THAT MAN	Waiting for a miracle: You never know when a bomb will fall on your head, a machine gun will wreak havoc behind your back; or some terrorists might take you as their hostage.

[*THAT MAN smiles with his mouth open.*

THIS MAN	Now you don't trust anyone who smiles at you.

[*The smile on THAT MAN's face disappears instantly.*

THAT MAN	Cats and dogs never smile.
THIS MAN	Only men are that cunning. They smile at you to tempt you, and if you take the bait, you'll be hooked for sure. Be careful when someone smiles at you. It means that he can't control you yet. When that happens, he won't need to smile anymore.
THAT MAN	Bah!

[*THAT MAN moves away. He circles around once to the back of THIS MAN.*

THIS MAN	The steps are so light and so silent, like a wolf's, or as if a vicious dog is about to jump up and tear at your throat.
THAT MAN	It's only your heart pounding. You're afraid of yourself. This happens to all the people all the time.
THIS MAN	No, someone's watching you, spying on you, and playing hide and seek with you. You son of a bitch!
THAT MAN	You were trembling because you still had a little feeling of shame left. You were trembling, which showed that

you were vulnerable. More or less you've still retained some humanity. Never mind integrity or the so-called "personality," you're so much more tangible, you're still living.

THIS MAN   I'll give you that. But so what?

[*THIS MAN lowers his head and looks at the piece of rope left on the floor. THAT MAN leans close to THIS MAN and whispers some instructions in his ear.*

THAT MAN   Pick it up once more. Pull on it and throw it away again. Everybody's the same, you think you can be the exception? Get used to people shouting at you. In front of big shots, you're no more than an animal, no matter how brainless those big shots are. And you, you let yourself be intimidated and controlled, which only proves your insignificance.

THIS MAN   You're such a worm, you can't push other people around, so you're destined to be pushed around yourself. Let me give you some advice: Whenever you see a crack, you'd better sneak inside and take shelter. For the sake of survival, you have to act like a wisp of smoke.

THAT MAN   Congratulations if you could be like that!

THIS MAN   You're not burdened by any principles.

THAT MAN   Lucky for you!

THIS MAN   You don't consider yourself justice personified.

THAT MAN   That'd have been so tiring.

THIS MAN   And you're not qualified to be a judge …

THAT MAN	Oh no! Who needs the misery? Of course not.
THIS MAN	You don't criticize others. You just want to show off a bit, offering your comments in a somewhat nonchalant manner. After all, you're an actor.
THAT MAN	Interesting!
THIS MAN	You're especially scared of blood. You avoid violence like the plague. When there are fights, battles, wars of any kind—between nations, between races, or between the sexes, you'll run at the first sight of blood unless, of course, it's a special effect in a play.
THAT MAN	Bravo!

[*The stage becomes darker.*

THIS MAN	In this murky darkness, you're groping your way around.
THAT MAN	You're getting weaker and weaker.
THIS MAN	If you shout, you'll lose your voice at once.
THAT MAN	In the face of the unknown, you're such a coward.
THIS MAN	Cowardice has nothing to do with it. Everybody is scared in the face of death. No one would commit suicide unless he was at the end of his tether and had nowhere to go. But then you're not at that stage yet, even though you're locked up in here and you can't get out. One hour, already one hour. The time passed so quickly. You're anxious and worried, you've fallen into an abyss, but whatever the outcome, there's got to be an end.

THAT MAN	Exactly. But how did you come to this? You'd made an appointment to meet someone, right? You missed the train at the station, that was all. But look at you now, you've been trapped, fallen into a quagmire. Even if you can get another train tomorrow, the person you were going to meet will have gone. There's no reason for you to travel any more. You've got to find another reason, but what reason can you find? It's still a question mark....
THIS MAN	A question mark. Let's say there's a question mark and let's say we're going to hang you on it, you'd still be going nowhere, no matter how hard you try. You might as well just leave it and let it be.
THAT MAN	There's got to be an ending. But it's not for you to choose. Just let nature run its course.
THIS MAN	Do you have anything more to say? Out with it! Now!
THAT MAN	Of course there's always something to say. It's a good thing that you've got so much to say, otherwise you'd have been dead, having died from asphyxiation. Look, we all have a brain, but if we were unable to utter even one word, then we might as well be dead.
THIS MAN	No, you can't let yourself be silenced! Your senses have already become more and more unfeeling, to the point of being numb. No, you can't let this happen, you can't become senile, you've got to shout and cry for help—
THAT MAN	Who would come to your rescue? What's the use?
THIS MAN	You keep muttering, but no one, except yourself, can hear what you're saying.

THAT MAN   Now you're even worse than an unfeeling stone, but
                    unlike you, the stone and its shadow are worth looking
                    at, no matter how or where you look at it.

                    [THIS MAN *is bearing down on* THAT MAN.

THIS MAN   And how about you? Pitiable worm, already a withered
                    corpse before it rots. You and your old bones, you're
                    just as good as dead. Oh no, you can't collapse, not like
                    that!

THAT MAN   That's nice to hear, but you can only sit there watching
                    yourself getting old and numb. You're wasting away,
                    and you can't do anything about it. Take a look at
                    yourself in the mirror: There's no way you can hide
                    your doddering old age. You run out of breath when
                    you walk, you're shrinking bit by bit, your final resting
                    place is your deathbed, from which you can't get up,
                    even when you breathe your last. There's nothing more
                    common, more banal than such an ending. And you,
                    you're still begging for your life; you've forfeited all
                    the dignity of being human.

                    [THAT MAN *moves away from* THIS MAN, *and moves farther*
                    and farther away.

THIS MAN   Man is such a fragile and insignificant creature. When
                    it all ends, he's only worth a few tears, which of course
                    are dependent upon other people's goodwill. Other
                    than that, how much is a life worth anyway? A tiny
                    little coin hardly makes a sound when it falls to the
                    ground. How can you force it to make some noise
                    when it drops? Might as well throw it as far as it can
                    go, then at least you'd get some satisfaction out of it!

Come, throw away what's left of your life as you would a small coin. If you have that impulse, it proves that you've still got some drive left in you yet. Don't wait until you're one foot in the grave, or when you've fallen into the grip of illness. Don't wait until you've lost your senses and control over your body. Put a speedy end to your misery while there's still time!

This isn't suicide because you finish him off yourself! The difference is: When someone commits suicide, he's hopeless and he gives himself up for lost; when someone finishes himself off, he is very much aware— he holds death in his own hand, he is in peace, and he's happy as he puts an end to his own life.

You're toying with death before its sudden arrival, as if you were directing a play—to put it more succinctly, a farce. Suicide is always a tragedy; when you murder yourself, it's bizarre, but it's also interesting, and you get some pulsating pleasure out of it, not unlike that of orgasm, at the moment of extinction.

[*This Man climbs up on top of a garbage can.*

You climb up the peak of your life for the last time. You afford yourself a bird's-eye view of this miserable world, and you put on a farce for your own enjoyment. Even though it's absurd and badly performed, it's also more wonderful than the boundless quagmire known as living.

[*This Man lowers his head and looks down, as dirty water streams from the bottom of the garbage can.*

The moonlight shines on your reflection, and your muttering is like the murmur of water in a stream. You feel the utmost sadness, you really want to weep. But heroes don't shed tears. Though you may not qualify to be a hero, you still don't resort to weeping and wailing. You put on a crying face only to ease your sorrows.

What's more, you've never been a hero, you've never fought for the masses, and you've never spoken up eloquently in any meeting of the masses on their behalf.

You still want to say that you're as far away from power as you are from the masses. Even if someone gives you some responsibility, at once you'll give it back to the person imposing it on you. No matter how big the power or obligation, you'll refuse them all, but then no one's ever given you any such appointment.

THAT MAN   Since you've wasted your life, let it be wasted from beginning to end.

Since life is worthless like dry shit, let it turn into a dreadful mess.

Since there is no salvation, death is the only solution.

THIS MAN   Let a cowboy become God!

And the Madonna a whore!

Let all this turn into an advertisement!

Chickens or cows, let them all go mad!

Let our Earth be polluted all the way!

Let the atmosphere burn in fury!

Let all geniuses move to the moon!

Let all the genes of all the races mutate!

Let all the weak die off one by one!

Before all this happens, before the new century makes people's blood boil once more, and before the crowd is once more provoked into a maddening rage, you first kill yourself.

It's like you invite yourself to a party, and you celebrate all by yourself. All your life you've been slaving away aimlessly and now you've reserved this short period of time for your own enjoyment. It's only normal, isn't it?

THIS MAN   Not only is it normal, it's absolutely right! You end your life at the right time, and you accept this in peace. This is ten thousand times smarter than a fly dying from slow suffocation inside a glass window case.

THIS MAN   Then why are you still hanging around here? If you've got anything more to say, out with it now!

THAT MAN   Am I in your way? If you want to put an end to your life, just do it! It's so simple!

THIS MAN   Then what are you looking at? There's nothing worth seeing.

THAT MAN   A strand of thread ... can't see it clearly ... drifting in the air ... still clinging to you ...

THIS MAN   Only you can see it, and only you think you can still see it, right?

THAT MAN	Exactly, that's exactly what you think.
THIS MAN	Go to hell!
THAT MAN	But you've never been able to get a grip of yourself. That's the story of your life, isn't it? Like a monkey trying to catch the moon in the water—
THIS MAN	Listen! Even if the water turns out to be a muddy puddle, imagine how wonderful you'd feel the moment you bend down and try to catch the moon!
THAT MAN	But you could only grasp a handful of dirty sludge.
THIS MAN	It doesn't matter. What matters is the pose! When you try to catch the moon, you actually aren't sure what you're going to catch. The fun part is the aesthetic pleasure you're looking for!
THAT MAN	You make something out of nothing, a tiny bit of meaning out of meaninglessness. It's not related to other people, but the feeling you evoke, it exists at this moment because you exist, and if you cease to exist, it'll vanish into nothingness.
THIS MAN	That's not your concern. You still consider yourself the center of everything. Your brief life just bestows on you this feeling of beauty, and the vast world is meaningful only in this small way.
THAT MAN	Oh, how wonderful!
THIS MAN	That's the truth. You search high and low, it's the only thing you've found, this miracle! You listen, you see, you feel, you taste, and you touch. You are happy yet in pain. Only in the process of muttering can your body and soul be confirmed.

THAT MAN	That's why you keep on talking to no end. Besides these words, what else can you leave behind?
THIS MAN	Shut up!
THAT MAN	Fine, then I'll say no more.
THIS MAN	Is God really dead?
THAT MAN	It seems so.
THIS MAN	And Jesus the Son of God died before Him?
THAT MAN	Very likely.
THIS MAN	No wonder, so many self-proclaimed saviors have popped up on our tiny planet. They've brought ruin everywhere.
THAT MAN	Now that you mention it, maybe that's why there've been so many disasters on earth.
	[*THAT MAN turns and walks toward the depth of the stage and disappears in the dark.*
THIS MAN	He's gone. That guy always looks in front of him, as if there were really something worth looking at. In fact, there's absolutely nothing on the other shore, not a strand of air, no wind, no impulse, no rhythm, no face, neither form nor words, neither color nor taste, and no feeling, everything is blurred ...
	[*THAT MAN reappears on the other side. A noose is lowered above the garbage can. THIS MAN takes hold of the noose.*
THIS MAN	In the face of this increasingly vulgar world, a world as degenerate as art, and in the name of a loser, someone

who has wasted his entire useless life away, you proclaim the death of this weak and helpless person!

[*THAT MAN walks quietly to the back of THIS MAN and helps THIS MAN put the noose around his neck.*

THIS MAN

Before the flood and the day of judgment, and before the angels sound their trumpets, you first kill yourself ...

[*THIS MAN closes his eyes. That Man lowers his head.*

THIS MAN

A fainting spell takes you to a never-never land ...

[*THAT MAN looks up, his face toward the audience. THIS MAN opens his eyes.*

THAT MAN

You swoon and you become intoxicated, just like you're having an orgasm. Why not? You poor fellow! You're such a jerk!

[*THAT MAN quickly pushes away the garbage can.*

THAT MAN

It's done at last.

[*THAT MAN looks at THIS MAN's body hanging in midair. Siren sounds.*

THAT MAN

They'll be coming soon.

[*THAT MAN slowly lowers his head. Motionless, he stands erect on the stage.*

Curtain.]

The French version was completed in May 2000.

The Chinese version was completed on New Year's Eve, 2003.

This play was commissioned by the French Ministry of Culture. The script was rehearsed and read by the Semaine de la SACD in the studio of Comédie Francaise in 2001. As part of L'Année Gao à Marseille *celebration in 2003, the play premiered at the Theatre du Gymnase in Marseille, directed by Gao Xingjian and Romain Bonnin.*

A Word from the Translator

When Gao Xingjian suggested to me to combine *Escape* and *The Man Who Questions Death* into one book, I thought that it was only a matter of length. Then it occurred to me, during the process of putting this book together, that the plays share between them a common theme—the fear of being trapped in an enclosed space. This spiritual claustrophobia is a recurring theme in many of Gao Xingjian's plays and fiction, a haunting presence in his life and art.

For a writer, Gao Xingjian argues, to escape is but normal, a fundamental desire to achieve total independence to think and to express oneself. As he says, to run away means to live and to preserve one's integrity. The inability to escape and thus to free oneself creates anxiety; in the same manner, the Gaoian neurosis is derived from the endless struggle for deliverance and the consequent horror of being stifled and dying of asphyxiation. In the two plays in this collection, the objective correlatives for encroachment are politics and commercialized art. Though they are real threats to artistic freedom, they are adopted as metaphors to represent the quagmire the artist finds himself in. If in *Escape* the characters are offered no exit in what our playwright calls "the tragedy of modern man," in *The Man Who Questions Death*, which he claims to be a black comedy, there seems to be a way out, even though one could only find cold comfort in the prospects of the final solution—killing oneself. As Gao himself puts it, the play is a "black absurdity."

My translation has become more flexible with time, that is, it has become less "visible." Of course, my "flexibility" could be other translator's "literalness," for I aim to translate everything in the source text, including referential and connotative meanings and stylistic features. In *Escape*, there are the now familiar Gaoian monologues, and *The Man Who Questions Death* is basically a soliloquy. All this relies to a large extent on rhythm and syntax to express emotive meaning and maintain energy on stage, which I have tried to reproduce in my translation.

The translation of the titles of the plays was also problematic. The Chinese title for *Escape* is *Taowang* 逃亡, literally meaning "escape" and "death." When the two characters are combined as a word phrase, the idea of running away is paramount; the meaning of "death" is usually extended to suggest danger, that is, the danger to one's life. I have been offered other translations such as *Fleeing*, *Absconding*, *Flight*, etc. I also considered *Running Away*. I finally chose *Escape* because it is more succinct and to the point, and it sounds more appropriate as a play title.

The translation of the title of *The Man Who Questions Death* was even more tortuous. Gao Xingjian and I discussed at length on the phone arguing back and forth and choosing among various possibilities, including *Quest for Death*, *Death Quest*, *In Pursuit of Death*, and *The Man Who Pursues Death*. The present translation is closer to the Chinese title *Kouwen siwang* 叩問死亡, and which I hope is more interesting without being overtly melodramatic. Here I would like to remind the reader, as Gao and I discussed, that the idea of "questing" is also important in understanding the play. (The play was first written in French with the title *Le Quêteur de la Mort*.)

I would like to thank Mr. William Evans, who generously donated his time and directorial expertise to make suggestions for changes to the draft, Dr. Finn Miller for copyediting, my son Ian for proofreading, and Ms. Shelby Chan of The Chinese University Press for editing the book, and for the many long hours she spent in selecting the wonderful pictures to grace the pages. She also translated Gao's "About *Escape*." Lastly I would like to thank Professor Mabel Lee for writing an excellent introduction to this volume.

G.C.F. Fong

List of Permissions

Permissions to use the following copyrighted materials in this volume have been granted by their respective copyright holders, to whom we wish to make our acknowledgements.

(*In order of appearance in this volume*)

Writings

"Two Autobiographical Plays by Gao Xingjian," by Mabel Lee. Copyright @2007 Mabel Lee.

Escape, translated by Gilbert C. F. Fong. Copyright@2007 Gilbert C. F. Fong. First published in Chinese as *Taowang* 逃亡 by Lianhe Wenxue, Taiwan, 2000. Copyright@2000 Gao Xingjian.

"Notes and Suggestions for Performing *Escape*," translated by Gilbert C. F. Fong. Copyright@2007 Gilbert C. F. Fong. First published in Chinese as "Youguan yanchu *Taowang* de jianyi yu shuoming" 有關演出《逃亡》的建議與說明, in *Taowang* by Lianhe Wenxue, Taiwan, 2000. Copyright@2000 Gao Xingjian.

"About *Escape*," translated by Shelby K. Y. Chan. Copyright@2007 Shelby K. Y. Chan. First published in Chinese as "Guanyu *Taowang*" 關於《逃亡》, in *Taowang* by Lianhe Wenxue, Taiwan, 2000. Copyright @2000 Gao Xingjian.

"Performance History of *Escape*," by Shelby K. Y. Chan. Copyright@2007 Shelby K. Y. Chan.

The Man Who Questions Death, translated by Gilbert C. F. Fong. Copyright @2007 Gilbert C. F. Fong. First published in Chinese as *Kouwen siwang*

叩問死亡 by Lianjing Chubanshe, Taiwan, 2004. Copyright@2004 Gao
Xingjian.

"A Word from the Translator," by Gilbert C. F. Fong. Copyright@2007 Gilbert
C. F. Fong.

Photographs

Plates 1 to 7 courtesy Gao Xingjian.

Plates 5 to 15 courtesy Alain Melka.

Paintings

Shadows # 2 (56.5 x 44.5 cm). Copyright@2001 Gao Xingjian.

Un Appel (98 x 94 cm). Copyright@2005 Gao Xingjian.

La Nuit paisible (133 x 115 cm). Copyright@2005 Gao Xingjian.

La Premonition (45.5 x 38 cm). Copyrigh@2005 Gao Xingjian.

L'Espace prolonge (73.5 x 72 cm). Copyright@2004 Gao Xingjian.

La Marche (74.5 x 97 cm). Copyright@2005 Gao Xingjian.